Common Sense

ABOUT MEN & WOMEN
IN THE MINISTRY

DONNA SCHAPER

◇

AN ALBAN INSTITUTE PUBLICATION

The Publications Program of The Alban Institute is assisted by a grant from Trinity Church, New York City.

Library of Congress Catalog Card #90-83136.

"You do not want the effect of your good things to be, 'How wonderful for a woman!' nor would you be deterred from good things by hearing it said, 'Yes, but she ought not to have done this, because it is not suitable for a woman.' But you want to do the thing that is good, whether it is 'suitable for a woman' or not.

"It does not make a thing good, that it is remarkable that a woman should have been able to do it. Neither does it make a thing bad, which would have been good had a man done it, that it has been done by a woman.

"Oh, leave these jargons, and go your way straight to God's work, in simplicity and singleness of heart."

Florence Nightingale
Notes on Nursing

To Carrie Tidlund, who wanted a man for her minister at first

CONTENTS

ACKNOWLEDGMENTS

I want to thank Warren, Nancy, Isaac, Katie, and Jacob, my family, without whose permission the early mornings could not have been stolen to write this book. I want to thank the many people in my several congregations who taught me how to be a minister and who forgot to put the word "woman" in front of minister after awhile. Also, I want to thank my own pastors who showed me a way to treasure the possibilities of parish ministry.

I want to thank Carole Brown and Anne Marie Coleman for being the kind of friends who are willing to read extensive manuscripts and not just read them, but critically react to them. I extend the same appreciation to Bob Pierce and to Kwame Osei and to John Nelson. Their friendship and their understanding of my work is very precious to me. The work of Jack Harris, Letty Russell, and Lynn Rhodes is very much the foundation of what I have done here. I hope I have built well on their previous insights.

Some of the material enclosed has been printed previously. I thank *Waterwheel,* vol. 2, no. 2, Spring-Summer, 1989 for their quoted article, "Agents with Integrity" by Mary E. Hunt. Their address is *Water,* 8035 13th Street, Silver Spring, Maryland 20910. Also, "Job Descriptions as Though the Gospel were True" is reprinted from *Action Information,* November/December 1989. Some of the material in the chapter "Deepening the Contradictions" previously appeared in *The Other Side.* Material from *The Duality of Human Existence* by David Bakan was published by Rand McNally and is here reprinted by permission of the author.

PART I

Men, Women, and Ministry

CHAPTER 1

Tiptoeing Through the Third Person Plural: An Introduction

I want to do something that will bother everybody. I want to generalize about men, women, and ministry. I have been taught caution in using the plural anywhere close to this trinity. As anyone will tell you, not all ministers are alike.

Men who have done a good job at pastoral ministry don't like to be lumped in with those who have not. Just because some men have made a mess of the ministry doesn't mean that all do. Women who can't climb the fence of prejudice that surrounds pastoring don't want to be lumped in with those who can. Just because some women overcome serious opposition and become good pastors doesn't mean that all women can or will. Some of those opposed to a woman pastor are right, but not for the reasons they think they are. Those opposed to allowing men to continue doing anything important are surely extremists.

Prejudice is stupid; it robs us of the chance to be genuinely critical by getting all the work (without any of the thought) done in advance. The many congregations that enjoy women in their pulpit do so because those individuals are good ministers and not because they are women. The same principle applies to men, right? Men who are good ministers are not ministers because they are men. They are good ministers by the grace of God and the community's consent in the laying on of hands. Plural voice regarding the ministry is, minimally, an interesting mistake.

To admit that you are going to be offensive and to use the plural in situations of minimal application is one thing. But then to spill more ink on the subject of ministry requires either a dedicated stupidity or an eccentric courage. I hope the latter is in play. We are far enough into the experience of men and women in the ordained ministry to poke up our periscope and look around. What is happening? Are different styles emerging? Some say yes in abundant and interesting doctoral dissertations. Gender is close to being *the* topic of the last decade. Others say no. People are people and ministers are a strange version of people and that's that. I suspect both sides have a piece of the truth.

One beginning of this book is in my appreciation for the work of Jack Harris in *Stress, Power, and Ministry*.[1] I thought perhaps there was a woman's point of view on these matters and set out to write it, but failed. It turns out that his point of view is already androgynous. Mine, I hope, will be equally so. Harris taught me that you can get in trouble in ministry by trying very hard not to get in trouble, and I have put that insight to use in drawing some generalizations about the pastor's authority, power, and stress. Where Harris connects arguments one to another, I connect story. I think of myself as one Margaret Hoisik, the stringer of pearls at Tiffany's. "Pearls should be restrung once a year," she said. "And if you wear them a lot, twice a year." I have some stories and experiences that I want to understand. They are the sequence of pearls. They tell a little bit of what is going on in this marginalized, famished, agonized, spiritually threadbare group known as Protestant clergy in the late twentieth century. The stories show us the paradox that we have been invited to dance during this long New Year's Eve party that will end the millenium. They name portions of our suffering and our joy. They demonstrate the differences of men and women as we experience some of the same things.

I probably decided to write this book over a decade ago when someone asked me if the clergy were more "female" or more "male" as a group. The question was so silly that it deserved an answer. Out of some spot in my soul that particularly loves a conundrum, I responded that it was clear that men who go into the ordained ministry tend to be more female, and that women who go into the ordained ministry tend to be more male. Therefore the profession must be the most androgynous of all. Or the most in need of psychiatric counseling. Or the most interesting perch from which to observe the gender tidal waves now washing over our culture. I pick the latter. Where else could we enjoy so much androgyny?

There is a plural here despite individualism's finest attempts to prohibit it. We are not just one, but also many; we are not only individuals with commitments, but a collection of commitments with individuals attached.

Both women and men in the ministry are hounded by the question of difference, no matter how stupid they consider prejudice. The nagging question of who's better is a competition both genders enjoy. The latest sexism is the bleary-eyed idea that a woman's natu-

ral gifts—specifically nurturing, relational gifts—make her ideally
suited for ministry. It is a lovely idea and, like most prejudices, true
enough to warrant its whispering. The consequences of such thinking, nonetheless, mutate into more trouble for women. The
"mommy track"—that pernicious idea that women will be happier
on a professional track below men because it will give them more
time for the children—and its consequent lower salaries are not far
behind such self-promoting logic.

Even so, there are some key differences between the sexes with
regard to ministry. To forget them is to put yourself in the way of
danger. For women, ministry is upwardly mobile; for men it is
downwardly mobile. This one factor invites all sorts of pretensions
by women, all sorts of anxieties for men. It shows up in women
having, in general, more hope for the profession right now than
men do. Such hope is tested when they reach their glass ceiling as
the most well-educated associate around. It is tested as they watch
men they went to seminary with serving congregations with a thousand members while they recycle their three hundred through the
same committees. It is tested as they come to terms with the advantages men have in the ministry by virtue of their being men. These
tests do not negate the upward mobility that ministry initially gives
to women. It is a real lift for awhile.

In light of these differences in how men and women experience
the ministry, I want to explore the matters of relative securities and
relative stresses. Are there different securities enjoyed by pioneers
and homesteaders? Different stresses? Are women as free as men to
fight in ministry? Why is it that if a man has trouble in his parish, he
has trouble in his parish, but if a woman has it, she is a woman
minister who is not quite working out? Is the way men have become professionals in ministry the correct standard for women?
How long will it take for women to graduate from the status of a
well-educated lay person into some notion of pastor? Do we want
to graduate? Is the competition between lay and clergy different for
men and women? Do vestments need darts at all or are our Roman
Catholic sisters correct when they declare that women becoming
priests means changing the priesthood? (I confess that I have trouble even writing the word "ministry" without adding professional or
ordained to it. Like the rest of Protestant culture, I forget from time
to time the priesthood of all believers and use the word ministry as
it is coded—the ordained ministry. I doubt that this usage is appropriate.)

In addition to the matters of difference and stress, there is the
matter of power. Power is one of those things so exquisitely in tension with grace as to keep most clergy permanently obedient to its

paradox. Which *do* we need more, power or grace? Can you have both? A man is stuck with power on the way in whereas a woman has to earn it. Not much power, mind you, does a man get, but just enough to trick him into thinking it is his right. Women don't think of power as their right. First, we get to be embarrassed for even wanting it. Then we get to be attacked in public if we show our interest. Then, after we get it, we get to feel guilty for having it. Power is one of those matters for which ordination does not and cannot prepare. Only by observant living does one learn its value; men get one set of lessons and, I think, women another.

Then there is the whole matter of authority. The Gospel makes it pretty clear that to follow Jesus is to know God. Women can do that and still be ignored. The stronger we are, the more likely are we to get in trouble. People are afraid of authoritative women, and if you don't believe me, watch all the qualifications women add to their statements. They are armor. The most astonishing difference between men and women is that men speak in sentences and women in questions. We refer to others in our very speech. We check out what we are saying by turning the end of our statement into a question mark. Men, on the other hand, tend to stand by the legitimacy of their own point of view.

These differences mean that we hear the Gospel with different ears. Each seeks to know and to represent God in speech and behavior. Some are more certain of their ability to do so than others. Men are much more severely tempted to think of themselves as God than are women.

The nooks and crannies I will explore in this book remind me of my problem with my lawn. It's going to be a long story, so get comfortable. It is one of the experiences I want to understand before I go to my grave. It all started when I decided to tread on masculine turf by purchasing a push lawn mower. The absolute hilarity of it all richly describes what has been my ministry as a woman among men.

I began by visiting every hardware store in town. I spoke to all the hardware store men, who in my view are even more manly than most men. They know both the standard and the unusual machines; their vocabulary is extensive. Wing nut, road hammer, ratchet, phillips screw driver roll off the tips of their tongues melodiously. When together, they speak in dialect. "I don't know what I'd do if a widget was stuck in my compressor. What would you do, Joe?"

Entering these male compounds is not always easy for a woman. You have the feeling that they smirk as you approach, that they amuse themselves with the innocence of your questions, that they both want to help very much and don't want to help very much, and thus are a bit conflicted when you make your request. (Yes, I am suggesting similarities with male clergy.)

Anyway, squirming enough to satisfy the hardware men's confusion, I said, "Do you have any push mowers?" Three times I was turned down. One said, between chews, that there wasn't much "call" for them anymore. He checked my ring finger before reluctantly offering to special-order one for me at the going rate of $90.00. Without the ring I feel I might have received more courtesy. The second guy actually laughed and said why would you want one of those things? The third man suggested that I try one of his power mowers. I told him that the very sound of a power mower made me think of more trips to the hardware store and the gasoline station and the repair shop and the consequent increase in my "nag" rating at home and that I didn't want all that involvement with power. He thought a lot of things about me that he couldn't manage to tell me right then. At the fourth place, the man said he thought he had one left somewhere and sure enough, he produced it, in a box, which I knew meant trouble. The box meant that it wasn't standing up, and if it wasn't standing up, that meant I would have to put it together, or nag my husband to put it together, and the whole point of this expedition was to keep him out of it. I just wanted to cut the lawn. I didn't want to have to take a whole course in screw drivers and bolts. (I am reminded of all the work you have to do to build a community before being allowed to do ministry with it.) So I told the salesman I'd take it if he'd find somebody to put it together. He said five dollars; I said sold. He said don't you want to see it first and I said of course not. I don't need to fondle it; I just need to use it.

If I were more of a person, while the three men were cautiously discussing the assembly and putting things together, I would have gotten out my nail file, sat on an air conditioner box, and done my nails. Just for the effect. But instead I took a walk around the perimeter of the store and waited for my machine. Fifteen minutes later, after the proper social rituals between the assemblers were performed and each had assured the other that they didn't know too much about these old machines "but," I was home and mowing. No muss, no fuss. No gas, no spark plugs. No husbands to program. My glee was girlish and unbounded.

Of course, I still had to face my husband who was going to be furious. What the bip bip bip bip bip bip is that, he predictably said. Don't you remember what happened with the last one? Etc. I did remember what happened with the last one. Sears kept it in their repair shop for over a year. I went there a half dozen times and did lasting damage to my blood pressure. Finally, they confessed that they had lost a part to reattach the wheel and that, of course, they didn't make those parts any more. Even with push machines, you can get into this sort of debacle. I could have cut my lawn with nail clippers in the time I devoted to arguing with Sears about the lost part and eventually the lost mower. My husband was not thinking of these things as he stared at my $90.00 purchase. He was calling me names, names that men have only for women, names that mean I am a jerk for not understanding or loving machines the way he does.

Both of my boys (but not my daughter) insisted on a turn behind the mower. I refused their request. Blowing hard, getting my heart rate way above its Wednesday morning aerobic level, I mowed the lawn. It was sheer bliss. Clack, clack, clatter, clatter. Except for having to move the curious kids out of the way, there were no obstacles. What I enjoyed most was the sound of the engine. There was no sound to the engine. None at all. There wasn't even an engine and thus there was nothing that I couldn't understand. Instead of feeling dumb, I felt smart.

Until my neighbor appeared. He came over and asked me what I was doing with a kind of disdain that I fully understood. He was upset that I was a nonparticipant in power as understood by men. He plays on my husband's team in these matters. Little does he know what a Luddite I really am. The Luddites smashed knitting mills in England at the dawn of the industrial revolution; they didn't want progress. They didn't want things to be easier. They didn't want things to go faster. They wanted their jobs and an appropriate technology.

Frankly, I'd prefer it if my husband would get around to mowing the lawn more frequently. Deep in my sexist past I think of lawn mowing as men's work. But he's working too many jobs right now to do that, so I get the draw. He thinks that requires my learning power machines, machines that I dislike on principle, in practice, and on the ground. Thus the push mower was a perfect solution. It got me "back" to a place where I could perform the task, where I could control it, where I could do it without assistance.

Anyway, my neighbor not only asked the question, he offered to come over the next day and redo the area I had done with his riding power mower. Yes, he did. When I came home the next afternoon, sure enough, there he was loudly riding over my mowed lawn. (I can't count the number of times this sort of thing has happened to me in committee meetings with male clergy.)

My neighbor mowed the lawn I mowed, my colleagues decipher what I say for male consumption. They think they are helping the

helpless, which they are not. They just don't like the way I do
things. Slowly. Quietly. Emotionally. Lots of failure involved. In a
way that sort of insults technology. In a way that allows children to
be near. In a fully relational way. I spent so much time observing
the various actors' reactions and feelings that I could barely keep
moving towards the lawn. I think this is typical of women to be
"stuck" so firmly in relationships that task is remote.

Whether the matter is mowing my lawn or practicing my profession, men seem to be everywhere. I wonder if they feel our presence as acutely. My mind is always full of male voices. Commenting
inarticulately. Telling me how to do it better. Explaining how it has
always been done. Writing their books in linear, rational ways. Helping me out while resenting my dependence. Helping me out while
being glad to do it—but I never know which is when, nor, I suspect, do they. The power relations between men and women are so
distorted by centuries of male versions of the issue that I barely
know how to begin to unravel what is going on when a lawn is being mowed or the men in the local clergy association are gassing
about something unimportant so endlessly that I really do think if I
were more of a person I would pull out my nail file. When men get
together, they don't really talk to each other or, if they do, it all
sounds like those two guys sort of putting my mower together for a
price. They don't talk about themselves but about "it," and yet anyone (female) can plainly see they are really talking about themselves. The "it" is a code, and if it's not, it really looks like one to a
woman.

Being a woman means that you care about the power relations,
about how the people feel as they interact. Thus matters of supposed simplicity complicate quickly. I can't even mow my lawn
without understanding how everybody else feels about it. All that
relating takes time away from the development of my lawn mowing
ability. That ability is male-version authority. I end too many of my
projects with a question mark. Even as I write here, you'll see me
jumping from layer to layer of first power, then authority, then
stress, then back again. It will be hard to decide which comes first.

The power to get your lawn mowed or to do just about anything
you set out to do eventually becomes a matter of authority. Who
says? By what criteria do they say? Do you have any say about what
the criteria are? I see the authority problem most clearly in raising
my children, two sons and a daughter.

Everything I can read on raising healthy children in a nonsexist
way encourages me to make sure my daughter has the privileges of
being a boy. Baseball gloves, pants, "cow-girl" hats, the works. I am
to make sure that she feels no barrier to the boys' world. Nowhere

do I read how to make sure that my boys have access to what it is like to be a girl. Nowhere. Nowhere are they taught to be as emotionally alert as she is. Or I am. Or as comfortable with connections. Or as content with sharing her toys. Or as happy with the quiet poke of a push mower. If authority is the ability to control yourself, to set and meet your own criteria, not someone else's, then these criteria matter.

I don't want to inflate the feminine or trash the masculine. I only want a two-way street. Right now my daughter is expected, as I am in ministry, to be able to do everything the boys can do, and then in her spare time, be a girl. A mommy. She is being programmed by a culture so anxious about gender that it can barely socialize its young, feminine and masculine. She is to expect no limit to her access to a man's world, whereas my boys are not even being invited into her world.

My daughter's Sunday school teacher corrected her the other day when she said she wanted to be a nurse. No, Katie, want to be a doctor, she was told. A two-way street version of equality would mean that if her twin brother announced he wanted to be a doctor, he would be told, no, Jacob, want to be a nurse.

Equality strikes me as a nearly ridiculous objective. All I want is a two-way street, a world in which the kinds of authorities that women have had and have would matter. Male clergy could be judged not just by their ability to be like men in ministry but also like women in ministry.

During my eighteen years in ministry I discovered an unwritten rule: I could have all the security and authority and power I wanted professionally if I could best men. Their ways have been the standard. I had to prove that I could use power and authority, male-style. No one ever wanted to know what power and authority might be, female-style. I could exercise that style in my spare time; men never stopped long enough to consider what such a style might mean for their ministries. I had to preach and pastor better than they did. That was the price of the ticket. When women have the freedom to be as lousy at the ministry as some men are, then we will have a two-way street. When women take the time to locate authorities and powers that are less masculine and more feminine, and men use and experience them as well, then we will have a two-way street. Between now and then, we explore the nooks and crannies of grace, aware that men and women are graded using different criteria. Men are graded on how well they do ministry the masculine way and women are graded on how well they do it the masculine way as long as they also remain feminine. It's a marvelous mess.

You will want me to say what is masculine and what is feminine. In the masculine world such clarity is important. In the feminine world, first you would tell me that you know what I mean. Then together we would explore the contrasts. We would do so in a way that allowed a lot of different right answers. Men would be very precise, objecting to this point and that point all the way to the prison of their own precision.

The lawn mower teaches me about differences and power; raising my children is teaching me about differences and authority. In that process I will learn all I can possibly manage about insecurity and stress. As I try to raise my boys to be more like girls, and sense very much that the culture is antagonistic and that I am a coward when it comes to putting my children through social trouble or using them as guinea pigs for what I know of liberation, I learn more and more about the authority of powerlessness, its detailed confusions, its momentary boldness, and equally momentary cowardice. About what Jesus meant when he said follow me. That we would get what we would need along the way but that it might not be there every second. Manna, mornings only.

In this increasing knowledge that more than a little risk is necessary, that in fact the commitments of ordination put at risk all that security is widely rumored to be, there is for me monumental, knee-shaking stress. My stress scale is permanently high. I don't know why it should be any other way. Stress is frustrated capacity, and my capacities are barely known much yet called for anymore/yet, if you get the drift of the eschatological tension in which I and many women live.

The risks are serious and Egypt is comfortable. Nobody minds in Egypt that I can use a man consistently to get my lawn mowed or that I have trouble finding my own God. Nobody minds that I fear that God is hidden behind a wall of male interpretations. In female Egypt, I am encouraged in these dependencies and obscurities. I am expected to be able to find a man to mow the lawn and I am expected to be comfortable with God, as distorted by men. (By the way, I am convinced that female interpretations equally distort and obscure. They would have to.) In my few baby steps out of Egypt, I have the audacity to mow my own lawn my own way. I search for a God that makes sense to me in my experience of slavery. That experience is different from what men have experienced: we think too little of ourselves while men think too much of themselves. Niebuhr called these differences the sin of pride and the sin of sloth, although he wrote volumes about pride and two sentences about sloth. He of course thought pride was a bigger sin than sloth; men think everything about them is "bigger" and thus have made it so.

Women also are paying for the presumptions we make about our own size: we assume we are small or at least smaller than men. Audacity makes us uncomfortable, and it makes lots of people uncomfortable, and women experience making others uncomfortable as a kind of disobedience. We are not supposed to do that: we exist to make others comfortable.

Unlike men, who are not all that comfortable with audacity either, women are terrified of it. Thinking of ourselves as important enough to deserve even a trip out of Egypt, much less the whole journey, feels like a joust with God. Or at least God as we have known "him."

Thus mowing our own lawn is deliciously naughty at the same time that it is safe. A man may come along and help us and thus deprive us of both the freedom and the terror of it all. Our wilderness involves these temptations, leaning on men, accepting their "help" in exchange for accepting their version of God. Oddly, we who are so very relational are asked by the Liberator to go it a ways alone. Like Jesus said, we can have whatever we can let go of. We can have our gifts of depending on each other as soon as we put that dependence at risk. Like Abraham with Isaac, a remarkably ironic story about a man fully engaged with his offspring, in ordination we vow to serve God and not men. We commit to the holy obligations and acknowledge as deeply as the Spirit allows us their tension with the worldly obligations.

Women are so good at serving men; men even say that that's what God wants us to do. Not to mention what happens to a mother's obligation to her children when she puts God ahead of them! With everyone back in Egypt—if not our own families as well—begging us to come home, we become well acquainted with the tug-of-war of risk. You do the dishes. I'll mow the lawn. Be a regular mommy, and we'll grow up to be regular boys. Women like idolatrous security and Faustian bargains as much as men do.

In ordination we pledge ourselves to rely on God, the God who for much too long has been a victim of male bias. Thus we really do not know (yet) the God on whom we must rely. We have to go out in a wilderness to find God and that requires the courage to bear loneliness. In that loneliness, we encounter our power and our authority, aware that all we need is not yet available but that God is near in the very risk.

What do women need? We need to have our capacities liberated. We need to stop the frustration of our capacities. We need to mow our own lawns and find our own Gods. We need appropriate tools. We need access to the criteria by which we will be judged. We need to be able to pass these criteria on as a heritage to our children. We need to understand our consistent return to the safety of the male wing, and we need to go there and rest when liberation is too much for us. We need names for our fears.

Of course, the problem is not all in our head. There are also external obstacles in the way of our fulfilling our holy obligations. Our insecurity is not only that we have an unfinished journey ahead of us. There also are enemies along the way. There are people who don't want us to break bread and pour wine. There are people who, while erroneously defending their own divines, find the attribution of holiness to women a form of blasphemy. These are the open enemies, the flag-waving enemies.

There also are some invisible, but no less real enemies. Many people think they have "no problem" with the ordination of women, but in fact have enormous problems with it. These people trip us up and don't even know why. Nor do we. We have so internalized sexism that sometimes we trip ourselves up as well. Women clergy are simply looked at differently, more like our virgin/whore mother than our distant father. Whatever feelings people have about their mothers—and most people, male and female, have enormously complicated feelings about their mothers, even more confused than those they have towards their fathers, which are confused enough—they also have about women clergy. Mothers are practically the only experience people have with female power. Put a woman in a vestment and it looks as if she has power; thus all the associations are maternal. These confusions trip up women clergy internally and externally and need to be understood, embraced, traveled through, laughed at. Our enemies will not be as motivated as we are to understand why they oppose us.

On our way to these reasonable responses to the confusion of womanly power, fear is our constant sidekick. I have told my women students who vow they are not afraid that they simply don't understand the situation. There is a key generational difference among women clergy right now, with the younger trusting way too much in the women's movement to guarantee security and the older generation much too burned by the trouble we've already seen. There are so many interesting ways to be mistaken.

I can tell you how the insecurity yearns for power by telling another story. I had the experience approaching the toll booth of the Tri-Boro Bridge. My four-year-old son was with me. An enormous truck wanted my lane, and I wasn't budging. As he tried to run me out of the lane, I landed on my horn long and hard. A cop came over to find out what was wrong, appearing at first very sympathetic. The truck driver got out of his cab, jumped down to my level, called me every name in the book, and then, for his finale,

hitched his dungarees up and shook his penis at me from, fortu-
nately, inside his pants. When he did this, the cop said to me, "Move
over lady, let's get going." My son was scared to death, particularly
of the truck driver who for a brief, quintessentially New York City
hot July moment, looked very much like he was going to hit me.
Aghast, Jacob said, "Mommy, why did that man shake his penis at
you?" I had no reasonable answer. Eventually I diverted his attention and said that the more important thing was that the cop yelled
at me and not at the truck driver. The whole experience was terrifying but not much more so than many other experiences I've had
with angry men where the danger was not just social but physical.
Men can use their power violently, and every woman knows it. We
don't experience physical fear daily in the ministry but in every
joust with men we remember who is "bigger."

The real difficulty in this encounter was having to drive the rest
of the way with my perplexed four-year-old who has more than a
passing interest in the matter of penises. I tried to explain to him
that penises were also gentle, made for having babies and bringing
love into the world. He didn't buy it for a minute.

As women clergy, the power we have is not strength. It is not
our ability to win the joust with God or the joust with men. Nor can
we borrow power in our continued dependence on men. Ours is a
battle with the waste of power; we are after the capacity we need to
keep our promises to God. The authority we have is our experience, our uniquely female experience. Authority is the ability to
control ourselves, to establish our own criteria, to rid ourselves of
fear.

The security we have is, frankly, minimal. There is danger. Its
root is sexism. Sexism is sin. So our danger is rooted in sin. The
root of sin? Ask your minister.

Someone once asked why the Equal Rights Amendment didn't
pass. People came up with astonishing reasons. Wrong time, bad
leadership, insufficient funds. The real reason the ERA didn't pass is
that sexism was, then, more powerful than efforts to overcome it.
That truck driver wanted my lane. The cop would just as soon have
given it to him. Even those on our side may not fight for us. There
is real danger, and we are crazy not to recognize it. It is like the
danger of racism: something about you that you can't change fright-
ens people enough that they hurt you. People of color understand
the danger in the "ism." Women are beginning to see and to understand why we also are often afraid.

I want to understand how women in ministry can live more securely in the midst of this insecurity. I want to at least recognize the
amount of stress our insecurity is causing. I'd like to walk up to it,

shake its hand, make its acquaintance, get over the innocence and hand wringing of being surprised by it.

So we embark in this book on our wilderness walk. Where in the desert are we on matters of authority? Of power? Part of what I have to say is that we are looking for security and authority and power in "all the wrong places." It may be time to take stock, now that we have left Egypt and are a bit on our way.

My companion in this stock taking is an odd one. I found myself listening to Mark Twain's *Life On The Mississippi,*[2] and making enormous connections between the life of a river pilot and the life of a minister—not a woman or a man minister, but a minister. The river gave me the metaphor for ministry I needed. You'll hear Twain's irreverence in the background and mine in the foreground. Maybe you'll also hear our reverence for the things we love.

NOTES

1. John C. Harris, *Stress, Power, and Ministry* (Washington, DC: The Alban Institute, 1977).

2. Mark Twain, *Life on the Mississippi* (New York: Harper & Row, 1883)

CHAPTER 2

Some Abbreviated Thoughts on Gender

I took my five-year-old son to the regular Friday morning meeting of our local clergy group. When we got there, he took a long look around the table and announced loudly, "Mommy, boys can't be ministers." His firm reliance on his limited experience is quaint and parochial; other prejudice is precisely the opposite. It is monotonous and public.

Women who behave in ways that prejudice does not approve soon arrive at a theory of gender. It is not an academic theory, but rather something we carry with us and use to abbreviate our experience. These abbreviations can be a mistake, particularly if they don't account for new data, but more likely they give the benefits that all theory gives. They explain and illuminate patterns, aggregates, repetitions. I will try to come clean on the theory of gender that I use so that I and the reader can be more ably critical of the distances we will travel together.

The sources of the theory seem important. In the simple task of mowing a lawn, I crossed into male territory where the rules are different, and I have to double my activity just to get through. Likewise raising my children. The activity involves insecurity, power, and authority, each functioning in a nonhospitable, if not antagonistic, culture. Likewise driving my car over a bridge. I have to fight for my lane. The sources of my gender theory are experiences like these, multiplied and considered a thousand times. They tell me over and over that men are different from me, that culture sides with men in what it values, and that sometimes it is willing to be extremely mean, if not violent, towards me and other women to get what it wants. I, of course, have this theory packed in my bags when I approach ministry and the doing of it.

If ministry were only a practical matter, like lawn mowing, these assumptions would have limited value. They would show us how men and women differ and would point to the bedrock dependencies most women have on most men. We could smile and shout, "Vive la difference." But our need for men has also encouraged us to trust male notions of God. We are dependent on that notion of God. Surely if we get stuck in the wilderness of our own spiritual journey, some man will come along and take care of things. Their way of raising sons will prove correct. They will change our tires, mow our lawn, drive our cars. Or so I think most women feel. At the bottom we want masculine saviors. To ordain a woman, and to ask her to know God and to do holy deeds, to marry, to bury, to baptize in the holy names, throws that woman into a tizzy on a potentially grand scale. Dependency is made a difficulty. That feels both liberating and frightening, both exhilarating and intimidating. It feels like conflict, like things banging up against each other. Such collisions rarely allow security in people. These conflicts grow into the prejudice of my little gender theory: we not only explain with it, we also protect ourselves. The theory is armor against difference, just like sexism is. In each case difference has the potential of being used explicitly or implicitly against women. Explicitly, with a cop pushing you out of the lane as though that were right. Implicitly, with a lack of disdain when you give your son crochet needles or require certain sensitivities from him before he returns to the playground.

In searching for God and speaking for God, matters of power become very important. Do you really have the power to go your own way? Can you really mow your own lawn or find your own God? Who says? Most women clergy, of course, will deny that they are speaking for God. They will end their statements about God with a question mark. That works for one leg of the journey, but not the other. We may be wise enough to know that all our words do not have divine inspiration, but most people, rightly, trust that some of them do. The hook of ordination is not easy to get off of.

The authority of our struggles gives us, by the grace of God, the power we need and therefore the security. I believe this is true for both men and women, but I think men assume more. Men have been taught to think that some powers and authorities come to them by virtue of their gender, and women have not. It's not that all men believe this, but they may if they wish. Women have a much straighter shot at the authority of our own struggles. We really don't have anything else.

It is useful to be more precise about the general differences between men and women, what I will refer to as the masculine and the feminine. I'm leery of putting any individual in either of these boxes. They exist as frameworks, not as people; aggregates, not points. Permission to even speak of gender principles requires some willingness to live along a spectrum.

David Bakan, in *The Duality of Human Existence,* provides a very useful beginning in gender theory. He associates the principle of communion with women and the principle of agency with men. According to Bakan, agency "manifests itself in self protection, self assertion, and self expansion; communion manifests itself in the sense of being at one with other organisms. Agency manifests itself in the formation of separations; communion in the lack of separation. Agency manifests itself in the repression of thought, feeling, and impulse; communion in the removal of repression. ... The very split of agency from communion, which is a separation, arises from the agency feature itself; it represses the communion from which it has separated itself."[1]

I have found it useful to address gender and ministry from within Bakan's larger framework because he uses it in a public and historical analysis as well. He sets out to clarify Max Weber's work on how integral the Protestant personality has been to the formation of capitalism. Bakan shows that there is an intrinsic unity of Protestantism and capitalism because both involve exaggeration of agency and repression of communion. I believe that agency unmitigated by communion results in the extreme privatizing of ministry as well.

Feminist ethical theory, with its focus on relationship rather than deed, is compatible with this analysis. To the feminists, the self is a rooted actor not an isolated actor. Carol Gilligan, in her ground breaking work *In A Different Voice: Psychological Theory and Women's Development,* notes that male experience highlights "the values of justice and autonomy" while female experience tends to emphasize the values of "care and connection."[2] Carol Gilligan is the theorist on whom I rely most heavily in making these experiential assertions about the differences between men and women in the ministry.

Probably these differences have at least one biological foundation. Nancy Chodorow has analyzed the differences in identity formation found between girls and boys based on the different responses to their mother, who is almost universally the primary caretaker of infants and young children. Young daughters grow to maturity in an enduring relationship with mother; they experience themselves as like mother. As a result "feminine personality comes to define itself in relation and connection to other people more than masculine personality does."[3] In order to define themselves as masculine, boys must break from their attachment to mother to achieve an identity independent from her. Male development thus requires greater individuation and stronger ego boundaries.

For me, personal stories give flesh to theories. The lawn mower experience will last long after I've forgotten the scholar's more significant work. Men mow the lawn without worrying so much about how to do it. They know how to do it and how to fix the machine that is supposed to do it. Lawn mowing is secure for them. They have the power and the authority needed to accomplish the task. The same is generally true of ordained ministry. Men have reason to believe that they belong in the profession. Women do not enjoy the same assurance and thus rely on more internal resources to do their jobs. Like the huffing and puffing of my lawn mowing, we have to work harder at it. We have more obstacles in our way.

Simultaneously we have an advantage. In being required to lean more heavily on our own resources, we have fewer institutions blocking us from God. (Yes, institutions can also help bring people to God. That is theoretically possible.) God's purported institutions may not legitimate us, but God does. We have learned that neither lawn mowing nor ministry is "men's work." We have also learned that different people cut grass in different ways. The advantage of such built-in pluralism allows us to love differently, if not better. The question of better doesn't really need to come up, but you can't have a theory of gender without it raising its head.

So, I'll come clean. I'm sure it's not right, but I do think of women as better than men. Better at loving, better at ministry, better at ascertaining multiple realities, better at juggling responses to those multiple realities. Better at lawn mowing because they don't use gas and make noise. Better at raising children because they can develop communion, which I think children need more than agency. Boys, I note, become men after they have "separated" from us, and then they cling most desperately to us as their only friends and confidants. Husbands, typically, need wives so much more than wives need husbands. I think women are probably worse at driving cars or hanging on to their lanes than men are, but I would probably do away with the whole automotive and highway operation anyway. Women would never have invented such a dangerous, expensive, individual transportation system in the first place.

Do I think I follow the Gospel's complex command to love by making these comparisons in this hierarchical way? No. Such comparisons are sinful. They are wrong. I am wrong in making them and keeping them so close to me. Am I trying to repent? Yes. But until culture and men give me more security, authority, and power—or I find a way with others to internalize those things in our own rival communities—don't count on a full repentance. I'm just not capable of it. I am put too firmly on the defensive by my daily experience. Repentance will involve getting me off the defensive long enough to allow for a meltdown of my protective armors. Right now I have every reason to defend myself, my children, my world from unmitigated agency, and only my sin as reason not to.

NOTES

1. David Bakan, *The Duality of Human Existence* (Chicago: Rand McNally, 1977), 73.

2. Carol Gilligan, *In a Different Voice: Psychological Theory and Women's Development* (Boston: Harvard University Press, 1982), 242.

3. Nancy Chodorow, "Family Structure and Feminine Personality," in *Woman, Culture and Personality,* ed. Michelle Zimbalist, Rosaldo Lamphere, and Louise Lamphere (Stanford: Stanford University Press, 1974), 44

CHAPTER 3

The Pastor as River Boat Pilot:
Toward a Theory of Ministry

One bad joke about male clergy is that they sit in the stands with the women and children watching the real men play the game on the field. Unpacking that insult takes a while. Women are passive; men are active. Ministry is not masculine, but feminine. Real, big, and good describe the public world of politics and economics; observation, children, and leisure all mark the private world of the home. By such simplicities, men and ministry are domesticated; they are kept in their place in the realm of Sunday School and private morality. They are kept off the fields of economics and politics. It may sound too stupid to really work, but in fact it does. Most ministry and most ministers are one-dimensional, domestic if not domesticated, content to watch with the women and children, here considered as one. Many obey their orders to stay in their place. Professional ministry in the U.S. is almost thoroughly privatized and feminized to the extent that ministers represent God. God appears to have a season ticket, to be thoroughly the property of the home team. My theory of ministry plays football *and* enjoys the stands. Many of us happily combine the public and the private, the pastoral and the prophetic, the political and the personal—or at least we try to. If my theory has any distinctive common sense, it is the combination of the female with the public. Again, it has the virtue of confusing most people. I don't sense that most women minister the way I do. Each of us has her or his own theories and experiences to make sense of, our own pearls to keep on the string.

Like all of us in the field, I have read volumes on theoretical approaches to the ministry. I know about the entrance at pastoring and the entrance at prophecy, the entrance of the king in governance and administration, and the entrance of the priest at the sacramental. Lately the entry ways are also marked shaman when they are not marked psychologist or manager. The spectrum is enlarging at both ends. Ministry is a mansion. Whichever door you come in by, public or private, mystical or practical, allows you access to many rooms, but not all. Nevertheless, men and women in ministry will be called at one time or the other to all the rooms. Neither football metaphors nor mansion metaphors even begin to contain the majesty of the full ministry.

I enter from the oddball. It would not describe what I do or why I do it that way to use pastor, priest, prophet, or king (ha). Nor am I a shaman and certainly not a manager or a psychologist. My roots are less in prehistory or Old Testament times than they are in culture, specifically American culture. I could describe my ministry as homemaking because mostly I behave like a housewife. That role, however, has been so denigrated that I doubt my entry point would satisfy most people.

So I turn to a person who speaks most deeply to me about the ministry: Mark Twain. He is a riverboat pilot, and I am an oddball pastor. We seem to connect.

In *Life on the Mississippi,* I feel Twain is describing ministry in the late twentieth century. His occupation is about to be rendered useless by the railroads. He lives with the knowledge of his own fading importance. He stands at the helm of his boat musing about how it used to be. The matters of stress and power and authority are central to his occupation. (Yes, the very entry of women into the field of ministry is an expression of the end of the profession. Ask any historian of the professions and he or she will show you how and why.)

Simultaneously, Twain doesn't see his work as the result of his own skills or efforts. He doesn't overrate the importance of his own authority. For him, keeping the river in good shape is even more important than keeping the boat or captain in good shape. For me, keeping the people in good shape is more important than anything. Through them the ministry happens or doesn't happen.

My major criticism of the ministry is this: I believe most pastors have neglected people over the years so thoroughly that only a precious few know the psalms or the higher criticism or how to organize a bake sale, much less how to become a community. I share Twain's joy in working on a good river. He describes the "pilot's paradise as a wide river hence to New Orleans, abundance of water from shore to shore, and no bars, snags, sawyers, or wrecks in his road."[1] What would happen if our people were ready to move towards God? What would happen if our days were not so filled with obstacles?

The preventive movement in medicine helps describe our condition. Our days as pastors are spent binding the wounds of a broken

community when instead they might be better spent forming a healing community. We are like the missionary who spends her days
downstream binding up those victims who float down the river. Preventive ministry would go upstream, diagnose, see that the problems begin in broken community and then go about the task of restoring community so that the numbers of victims might be
reduced. Twain took better care of his river than most of us do
ours.

When Twain describes the excruciating process by which he
learned to pilot the river, I identify fully. I am not joking or indulg-
ing the cliche when I say that I still don't know how to do my job
as pastor. I am not yet fully taught. In teaching public ministry, I so
frequently stand in awe of what it is that we are to become, that giving up seems quite sensible. Twain's description of his tutor's tricks
goes on for fifty or sixty pages. Here is what he experiences when,
having accomplished a particularly good turn, his tutor tells him
that he has more to learn:

"Then I've got to learn just as much more river as I already know?"
"Just about twice as much more, as near as you can come to it,"
replies his tutor. They talk.
"I think I was a fool when I went into this business."
"Yes, that is true. And you are yet. But you'll not be when you've
learned it."
"Ah, I can never learn it."[2]

Later Twain explains the difficulty again:

When I returned to the pilot house St. Louis was gone, and I was
lost. Here was a piece of river which was all down in my book, but
I could make neither head nor tail of it; you understand, it was
turned around. I had seen it when coming upstream, but I had
never faced about to see how it looked when it was behind me. My
heart broke again, for it was plain that I had got to learn this
troublesome river both ways.[3]

Twain refuses to romanticize the situation. He knows that in the
old days, during the war, the pilots enjoyed more popularity and authority. But he comments dryly on this nostalgia. "There was a
young New Yorker who said, what a wonderful moon you have
down here." The response, from the old timers who thought everything used to be better, "Ah, bless yo' heart, honey, you ought to
seen dat moon befo' de waw."[4] This strikes me as good advice for
the ministry in decline: humor the situation.

Twain would never admit what a good socialist he was either. The organization of the captains into a union so that they could collect a decent wage was really the only sensible response to the threat of their decline. Alone they could only suffer.

Oddly, Twain thinks that memory is the highest gift of a pilot. I would imagine that is true at the level of skill. If we can learn from what we have heard, if we can say to a person, ah, yes, I have met you before on the river, perhaps we can be of use to them in their navigation. Yesterday I used memory all day long. Without it I would have been totally overwhelmed instead of almost so. I heard a story about adultery in high and embarrassing places. Then I was asked to fish out a kleenex from an 87-year-old woman's diaper. (Yes. It was her trick for the nurses so she wouldn't have to sit in the hall all morning in her chair. She knew they wouldn't have time to change her. The kleenex, like so many illusions, started to offend her old bones.) I consulted with our treasurer 100 times (I exaggerate) about details he should have understood. I organized the follow-through on a protest against incineration. I prepared the bulletin for Sunday's service, taped a TV interview, delivered money to the food center, information to the shelter, stopped at the school to visit one of my members who is a kindergarten teacher with twenty-seven in her class (yes, that is illegal), made one call on a widower who said he would never marry again because he never did know what you were supposed to talk to a woman about (!), visited a key lay leader whose appendix ruptured on the day her husband was moving out and their separation beginning, and saw a few spots along the river that I had never seen before. And this is just what shows up at the level of my calendar. We remember these days. We don't think of them as odd. We store them and they become our passage down the river. They are a public process, like Twain made navigation a public process, the matter of getting from here to there.

The details of ministry are equally as important as the details of piloting. Twain went 400 pages and almost never philosophized or theorized; he just described the turns in the road.

I will rely on Twain to convince you of the importance of a narrative style and to remind you that it is not just women who understand things pearl by pearl. When I theorize about ministry I want to do so in the spirit of Twain. Wry, humorous, accepting of the realities of the situation, always trying to get from one point to the next without hitting too many snags. The better pilot prepares the river, the better pastor prepares the congregation. We don't enjoy their difficulties in living, we emphasize prevention. We don't just feed the poor, we try to change the systems that create the poor.

This is what I mean by public ministry: it is those things done collectively to move us closer to God's promised time and commonwealth. Moving on down the river is always more important than the time we spend getting our boat unhitched from a sandbar. Did the one day I described show this emphasis? No, it did not. Theories show us our destinations; stories show us where we are. Common sense reports the interaction.

The limitations in my understanding of ministry show up in the theory's sources. It is too American. I understand the urgency for community the way Twain understands the upper river because I have lived my entire life in a situation of broken community. Much is promised to the American, as if all life was the homecoming game and its multitude of good feelings, but little is provided. Our economic and political life is built against community for individuals. In it, the stronger wins, the weaker loses, and the men on the field tell us this is the way God wants it. Thus I minister always in conflict with the culture, with my central purpose being the restoring of community—sacramentally, as a sign of God's real intentions; prophetically, to gain power; pastorally, to heal people of their own divisions and those laid upon them. Community is both end and means. The governance category is actually the trickiest, perhaps because we have freedom on paper in this country and perhaps because the paper refuses to describe what is really going on. The Constitution imagines a covenant, but it is broken.

As one who idealizes community, I have to understand power and I have to understand conflict. These two matters become my expertise: they are what the river teaches me over and over. Because I travel back and forth so often, I end up learning about power and conflict the way Twain understands the bends in the river. Perhaps some stories will show how my river flows.

A Unitarian congregation in New Jersey started an unusual housing project. They gathered a dozen single elderly into a large Victorian home. It was a step between a nursing home and the people living all by themselves. When asked what was the best thing about the arrangement, one of the women said, "If I feel like I want to bake a cake, I can go down to the kitchen and make one. And, even better, there are people there to eat it." The Gospel is obsessed with the Christian's responsibilities to others. We are to invite the poor, the maimed, the lame, and the blind to our table. Not, mind you, to the local service center, but to our own tables. We are to feed the hungry and clothe the naked not just through the local Council of Churches, but through our own cooking, out of our own capacities. The poor themselves are not exempt from these responsibilities. If you live in a church-supported housing project, long after the time has passed when you can pay your own way, you are to make cakes. You are to make them for others. You are to enjoy what you can do for others whether you are poor or rich. No class is exempt from the claim to do justice. This story shows how the pastoral can become public. Too often we think of the pastoral as everybody getting their own little canoe down the river safely. The pastor administers all this care. Instead, I think of the pastoral as the development of situations where people can exchange gifts and be useful to each other. It is a public ministry to make these exchanges of resources; both sides of the equation win. The vehicle is community.

Sacramental ministry can be understood in a public way as well. I attended an art exhibit at Williams College in Massachusetts called "Stitching Memories: African-American Story Quilts." Over one hundred patchwork quilts are on display, made by slaves or slaves just freed who had stopped at one of the Underground Railroad stops. Stitched on the fabric are maps. They show the way to freedom, the way north. You can only see the map after you're told what to look for. The tiny pieces of extraordinary fabric point a clear way to justice and freedom. Preaching is stitching a quilt, showing people how to get home. Liturgy is one of the maps people have made over time and continue to use because it works.

Prophetic ministry is so often understood as the separate sphere of the social action committee. Or it is "issues." When understood as part of the larger navigational plan for the community, prophetic ministry becomes almost antagonistic to issues and services and projects to "save" the poor or the useless or the frail. Consider that grand rubric, "What's wrong with youth today?" My answer is that we don't give them enough to do that is important. Prophetic ministry is making use of people to the glory of God. Youth become mature physically long before there are social uses for their maturity. Something like a volunteer or mandatory youth service corps where instead of shooting at each other on Bensonhurst streets young people could work together to rebuild bridges or clean up violated areas or mix it up—like they do in war—would go a long way towards providing them a sense of usefulness. I think we should send all stranded teenagers away *to peace* as soon as they reach age eighteen. Don't let them come back for two years and certainly don't let the richer ones go to college until then. Not until they bake a cake and find others to eat it. The goal of prophetic community is to restore broken community, to restore streets in which to dwell. It is the strangest triumphalism that causes Protestant mainline churches to think that we have to do this *for* others. So much of our prophetic ministries have turned into trumpets to blare our own importance to the world. So few of our ministries have rebuilt community. Most have actually hurt community. We keep youth useless by putting them in programs we design for them. We keep old people useless by baking cakes for them.

There are at least two kinds of shelters for the homeless: one where staff are paid by the state as professional social service workers, another where the homeless themselves take care of business. The shelter in my former church was closed down by the State of Massachusetts in the late 70s because we were "letting" the homeless do too much themselves. Governor Dukakis wanted to give us $600,000 to professionalize and regionalize the shelter. We refused this "gift" from the state. How dare we refuse the gifts of the poor, we whose main complaint is that we are so busy? How dare we set up a world in which frail people who wake up with the energy to make a cake can't find anyone to enjoy it with them? Tom Wolfe humors WASPs along in his latest novel, *Bonfire of the Vanities,* when he calls his nonhero a master of the universe. So much of our prophetic ministry has been done from this perspective that community has been broken rather than braced. It is really the intrusion of our private assumptions about ourselves and our positions in the universe that has intruded into our public work and made, too frequently, a mess of it.

In pastoral ministry, when I do all the giving and my congregation does all the receiving (or we begin to perceive things that way), a mess begins. I misrepresent the Gospel. I teach people how to stay safely miserable rather than how to head north. I teach people how to eat rather than how to bake. I relate to God on their behalf. This one-way street of ministry is a real set up. One metaphor is that of being a wife and mother in an unjust home, another is being a person of color in a world that thinks of white as useful and other colors as useless. Because of its correspondence to the common injustice of our domestic situations, women are sorely tempted by imbalanced ministries. We are also keenly aware of them. Ministry is not baking in the kitchen all day long. It is partnership with the map makers, those who are finding their way north. Some baking is done by us, but never all. Our ministry will be fruitful to the extent that we can balance givers and gifts and learn to be partners with both.

In matters of the pastoral and of the prophetic and the sacramental, public ministry focuses on broken community and tries to restore it. If we can get our own conceits out of the way, things improve rapidly. In matters of governance, our purpose is to keep government on a human scale. We need to keep the big out of the way of the small. We need to open up space for the local and not let the global sweep it off the map, mentally or materially.

Therein lies my beef with the environmentalists. The hot word lately is *planetary*. This word describes a problem in a way that can't be solved. In fact, though we now have serious problems nearly everywhere on the planet, we have no problem that can accurately be described as planetary. There are no national, state, or county problems, and no national, state, county, or planetary solutions. This business of hiding in the large-scale solution to small-scale problems serves mostly to distract people from the small, private problems that they may have the power to solve. When accurately described, all problems are private and small. The problems are our lives. We live, all of us, either partly wrong or altogether wrong. It was not just the greed of corporations that decided the fate of Prince William Sound; it was also our demand that energy be cheap and plentiful. The economies of our communities and our households are wrong. Can you consider it any other way when you take out your trash? When you open your favorite cookie and realize that it takes two minutes to get into the package, so cute is it, and that it took three days to be trucked here from California where it was baked? When you turn the key in your car ignition and deplete the ozone? When you get your morning coffee and all they offer is a styrofoam cup? The answers to these problems are local not global. They have to do with buying our food and being satisfied with what we can grow here. Which do we prefer, doing without orange juice or global warming? There are choices. They have to do with changing our modes of transportation. They have to do with carrying our own cups around and washing them. They have to do with memorizing our own piece of the river so that we know it by heart. These are the solutions. If these are not the solutions, then there are no solutions. There are only problems, planetary problems at that.

Wendell Berry, a poet in Kentucky, states that for a long time all the people in his community who made decisions were outsiders either in their mind or body or both. The government thought big thoughts from far away and sent memos telling them what to do. The schools prepared children for the "world of tomorrow" which everyone hoped would be suburbia. The church, he says, is present in his town. But both local congregations have been used by their denominations for almost a century to provide training and income for student ministers who do not stay long enough, he says, to even be disillusioned. The major institutions in most towns have not been *of* the town and its people; therefore they have not tried to perceive the good possibilities that are there. No one is wondering on what terms a good life might be lived there, a life not disconnected from the large-scale, but rather connected on a community basis. The question that must be addressed is not how to care for the planet but how to care for each of the planet's millions of human and natural neighborhoods, each of its millions of small pieces and parcels of land, each of which in some precious way is distinct from the others. Our understandable wish to preserve the planet must be reduced to the scale of our competence. The scale of our competence is local not planetary. We are each one, not many. We are each capable of small-scale love. Love on this scale is a beautiful thing. It is heroic only when it is compelled to be.

The great obstacle to local rather than planetary thinking is that we have the conviction that we cannot change because we are dependent on the very thing we're told is bad for us. We cannot stop driving our cars because we are dependent on their freedom of mobility. We cannot give up orange juice five months of the year because we are dependent on it. If that is not the addict's excuse, then I don't know what it is. The very language, the very flow, the very diagram of the sentence is the excuse of the addict. We cannot change because we are dependent on what is wrong. Don't think I don't take these addictions seriously. I don't walk to church mornings either. We are each only sort of committed to our best ideas.

And thus I point you to the *sort-of* nature of ministry, the small-scale nature of its possibility, to what faith might be in our times. We cannot guarantee to Jesus that if we care for this world by caring for our community that we are going to be able to finish the job. We don't even know ourselves if we have the energy to lay the first stone, to give up our second car, to buy a bicycle, to buy local food, to change our point of view on the subject of how we conduct our own household affairs. I, personally, am very attached to ziplock bags. We don't even know if we can take the first step. How dare we promise more than that?

The only big gift we can offer to Jesus is our human scale of competence. To pilot our piece of the river as well as we possibly can. To get all hung up in the details and the changes in that piece of the river. See what happens if and as governments and churches and schools begin to care about what happens here and now. If we live more like Main Street and less like interstates. If we back these choices with dollars and not just desires. Ministry may begin in a grandiose love, but it ends with a commitment to the local. Because of this, I have never been able to love any other kind of ministry as much as I love parish ministry. The local is so richly loved there.

In Chicago there's something called Project Self-Sufficiency. Five hundred welfare recipients will enroll in a program at St. John's Lutheran Church on the West Side. Before they are given their check each month, they will be involved in a support group, a job training program, and volunteer work at the Bethel New Life Center, which is at the church. After they have made friends through these projects and their peers have certified the friendships, the check will be given out. When asked if she would like to expand the program, Mary Nelson, the director said, "GOOD GOD NO. Don't you think 500 people are enough to form a human community? They're trying to give us people from outside the neighborhood and we don't want them. We want to be able to see and touch each other, that's all. Please leave us alone with your ideas of expansion."

We can see more of the WASPish addiction to our own size and importance by relistening to President Bush's speech on drugs. He smiled too much during it. Or at least that is what the social worker told me who made a point of watching the speech with a dozen addicts with whom he had worked. Yes, he watched the program with the people who were being talked about. They said that the ideas sounded okay, but that Bush somehow seemed happy about delivering them. How could anybody be happy about addiction? Easy, I thought to my cynical self. When the problem is somebody else's and not yours and your job is to make a lot of decisions and be very important and spend a lot of money and manage the war between the agencies who want to spend all the money, that kind of power makes you happy. It is global. It is feeling global. But having no power at all—that's what drives many people to drugs in the first place.

We need to get beyond TV power and live as though there were different kinds of power around. Different ways to be important than getting to the top of something and sitting on it. Instead, we could make a home and find a community. We could be loyal to what we have made. We could put the interest of our community first over our own interest. We could love our neighbors, not the neighbors we pick out, but the ones we have; not the church council we pick out, but the one we have. As far as possible, we could make our lives dependent on a local place, a region, a neighborhood, a household, a congregation, each of which thrives by care and by generosity. We could make our lives independent of the industrial economy, which thrives by doing damage. We can find work, if we can, that does less damage. We can enjoy our work and do it well. These things are all within our power. They will bring us happiness and peace.

I know that a theory of ministry should be more formal. It shouldn't confuse the pastoral with cakes nor the prophetic with rearrangements of the rites of passage for youth. The sacraments are certainly more than quilts made by slaves and the matters of governance surely are bigger and more complex than I can begin to understand. Ministry is not just riding a boat down a river with people who want to get back home—and as soon as they get home, want to get out to see a little something different.

I guess I am understating the matter on purpose. People with American sources for their theories and their experiences are so much more likely to overstate so perhaps I am compensating.

At least I got rid of the football metaphor. It was too much about leisure, and ministry is work. It was about separations and agencies. Rivers flow. But, I didn't completely let go of the housewife and her homemaking task. Like football, it is too gender-bound to accommodate the androgynies necessary for the journey, but the metaphor describes some of what happens in ministry. If only all of the things that we consider masculine properties and all the things we consider feminine properties could be used in our ministry on the river, and then a few more. For the pilot, both agency and caring must be fully in play to navigate well.

Like Twain, I stand in awe at the majesty of the river. The only protection I have from completely romanticizing it is to report it. I will report from the pilot's point of view concerning matters of increasing stress, decreasing authority, and the enormous need for power that local communities must have to thrive. I'll try not to overdo it.

NOTES
1. Mark Twain, op. cit., 195
2. Ibid., 78.
3. Ibid., 34.
4. Ibid., 180

PART II

Security

CHAPTER 4

The Places We Won't Find Security
—and Why:
An Introduction

In the first parish where I was the solo pastor I came home
from work so excited with what had happened that I regularly en-
tertained my husband with tales of awesome human experience.
Before being told these tales, I knew life was interesting. But I had
no idea how interesting. I had no idea just how much living was
going on.

I'm talking about both the walk-ins and the regulars, the members and the vast army of uninvited guests who show up as soon as
word hits the street that the door is open. What some of my members would tell me about their lives left my jaw permanently askew.
Incest. Internecine robberies. The sheer number of years some of
them had already put up with violent spouses. I had an eerie kind
of appreciation for having such a front-row seat on human life. Call
it voyeuristic, if you will. It was exciting to know what was going
on. I think men in ministry hear the same things, but perhaps
women get to overhear more about sexual violence. It doesn't matter who hears what. What matters is that ministers hear too much.
Our perspectives are mightily skewed. We see more than we can
bear seeing.

Since these first few years my excitement has dwindled. I am not
as awed by a whopper of intergenerational trouble or what Johnny
did to Sue to get drug money. Then again maybe I am as awed, but
the awe has gone underground into some repressed cave where I
am storing all the matters in my vocation about which I can do
nothing. The stories began to scare me. I became and remain overwhelmed by the mountain of human need that God's caring
through God's representatives has targeted. Ability to think more
systemically has only exacerbated the problem. Each time one of
these whoppers walks in I see the racism and the sexism and the
effects of the commandment to move up in the world. All the fear

of the other, the fear of not making it on your own are part of the trouble pastors hear day in and day out. That one is supposed to do something about any of this is unspeakable.

Thus my welcome into the uncomfortably passive place where we wait on the Lord. The result of this excitement turned awe turned fear, and its frequent switching of emotional positions has required that I seek security in waiting vigorously on the Lord. There has been no other place to go. I have had to convince my-self, over and over again, that solving this mess is not up to me. I think men skirmish on the same borders. Ministry requires that we release responsibility for those for whom we care, that we learn to care for them without demand for improvement. If we do not learn to live without results for our labors, we spend too much time working the false securities. We are too desperate for the external demands of salaries and status and too much suckers for the latest gimmick and latest ministerial technique. We try too hard to "do something."

The puzzle becomes clearer if we think about one simple matter, that of referral. You would think, given our limitations both of time and ability, that referral would be a good idea for clergy. Sometimes it is. It is good for us to dwell among partners—professional coun-selors and other experts in various exotic difficulties. But it is also good for us to take weakness and difficulty into our parishes. This puzzle works on the same axis as that of security. After (or while) we try all the popular referral locations, we discover that they are not going to work and that we are really on our own with God if we want safety and satisfaction in the ministry. It is our very accep-tance of our weakness that locates our strength.

I have no doubt that my ministry is better and fuller and more capable of caring when I am leaning on the everlasting arms, and that my ministry is punier and stingier when I am not. My experi-ence is simply too clear. Sending away the poor and the hungry and the weird from our doors—"doing something"—and sending them to the state or the psychologist or whatever refuses the real strength of the parish. The burial of my internal demons in some cave has the same result. The parish's real strength is its ability to care nor-mally, as opposed to professionally, for such people and for such turmoil, mine and yours. When we send people away or bury tur-moil, sometimes we are sending our weakness away. We don't want to see it around, nor do we want to see the face of Lazarus in drunks who stay drunk or the poor who stay poor. When we cam-ouflage our own failure to represent God's love by filling our wal-lets or our calendars, in technical approaches at up-and-coming in-stitutions or wherever, we refer our weakness to a place that can't hold it as well. When we send our weakness away, sometimes, the trick is on us. Our strength goes with it.

We look for security in all the wrong places. Agency unchecked by communion is idolatry at work: Let's do something, it says. Let's act for God. Let's be God's substitutes. Both men and women in ministry are mightily tempted toward idolatry. After all, we stand in for Jesus at the table, at the altar. Sometimes we forget we are but mortals. What follows is an exercise in understanding idolatry and how it compounds the very stress it is promising to reduce.

CHAPTER 5

Beyond the Mayflower Approach to Ministry

As all of us who have tried to achieve it can tell you, upward mobility is not our security in the ministry. So much of the advertising budget of the culture is spent on convincing us of the opposite, that upward mobility is our only security, that we are foolish not to direct all our energy in that pursuit.

My favorite picture of our American mythology is the Mayflower ad. We move from a small apartment to a larger apartment on to the smaller house and then eventually to the larger house, with a Mayflower van taking us through all the prescribed squares. Clergy could redo the ad by simply substituting churches: small, medium, and large. Men are tempted to feel bad about their ministries if these progressions don't occur; women are not so much so, yet.

The reason is simple. Bigger churches don't want women. We are for them a step down, and they don't want to disobey Mayflower either. It is not that women don't want to move up. We do. Some of us want to move up desperately. Nor are we immune to the considerations of the ladder. We are probably already enjoying the upward motion of our status in our 100-member parish. For women, ministry is itself upwardly mobile; for men these days it is just the opposite. If all your life you think that you might become a secretary, and then you have a secretary, the sense of flight is immediate and gratifying. Again the culture prepares us well for such voyages, with ministry in the moment being kind to women and cruel to men.

Men are not enjoying the downward mobility that ministry now offers most of them nor do they appreciate the competition of women. We are winning more jobs now than we used to. Our very entry into their field has pushed the field down a notch in status. Soon it may go the way of library work or teaching and turn into one of those service fields where only courageous men dare go.

I remember applying for a seventy-member, "dying" urban church once in Philadelphia. I really wanted that church. I liked the people, the neighborhood, the whole scene. I was thirty years old with six years experience in the ministry. I had been fooled by my "first woman" affirmative action positions at the national level of my denomination into thinking that I had an outstanding resume and some significant experience. I couldn't imagine not getting the call until the grapevine informed me that the position had been given to a twenty-three-year-old who would graduate from seminary that year. The difference between him and me was that. He was a him and I was not. The experience was worth its weight in gold: I learned that I alone as an individual was not going to make a flying leap over the fence of sexism. I learned the difference between public and private, structure and individual.

Since then I have heard this story a hundred times. Congregations don't want to play the upward mobility game with women in the same way that they want to play it with men. Some of us may be associates forever. More and more congregations are attracted to the mom-and-pop ministry, especially if pop is senior over mom. Women are much sought after for the second seat of associate already.

These exclusions from the upwardly mobile track may prove to be enormous blessings, forcing us to locate security elsewhere. I left one parish for a variety of reasons, not the least of which was that the salary couldn't stretch to meet the cost of housing in the community. Even with their generous increases, I couldn't imagine the stretch. The woman who followed me came in at a level so much higher than my leaving level that I gasped for air at the very thought. She must have said something to them. I didn't have the courage—not with piety so deeply etched in my ministerial soul. Ministers don't do that sort of thing. Certainly women didn't either. What if I had been able to ask for a salary increase

It may be anathema or a heresy or both, but I rather like the taboo against ministers asking for a salary increase. My ambivalence about money could not be more thorough if it tried. Yes, I know it helps the cowardly parts of my piety and my womanliness not to have to obtain such courage. But here's my argument. Asking for money is a Mayflower approach to ministry. It is too "affirmative action," in the worst sense of that abused term. Too contractual. Too untrusting. I think beyond the categories of the moment that there is covenant, there is something relational to ministry. I think if/when women gained access to the power to determine professional criteria for ministry that our ministry among people would be better, people would minister to us. I'm not sure. I am just hooked on those kinds of hopes. I wager they will give me more security than settling for the way things are. Men could partner with us in these risks, but I'm not counting on it.

I understand what a congregation is saying when one of its members whispers to another at the bake sale table that "she" actually asked for more money. I understand the hiss, the hurt, the gossipy denial of the status of *person* to their minister. I understand their disappointment that their minister is acting like everybody else when they wanted to see a little more unworldliness. I don't approve of ministers being set up to do God's work while the lay people ask for increases in their salaries. That's not the point. Rather I think we are looking for evidence somewhere in our world of a trackless path, an even as opposed to an upward stride. We are looking for evidence that God will provide. I'm certain that it is not up to women or clergy to provide that evidence; we have enough to do. But I would be interested in a world where men and women clergy figured out how to be financially secure without breaking covenant with the congregation.

I imagine an association like that of the steamboat pilots. We get together. We set rates for our services. We control the front door so that seminaries don't foolishly stoke their own fires with unnecessary competition for us. More importantly, we set some of the standards for ministry and take that power away from the seminary and the congregation. To be sure, the congregation still calls. But we get in on the pool of people whom they may call. It is at the social level that salaries get set, not the individual. Such an association, dealing as it would with the real issues of money and standards, might actually feed some of the perennial hunger clergy have for security or friends or fun or a place to go when you have to stand over against your own people, or a place to go where others might review, consider, evaluate your work. We need a counterpoint to the hegemony of the seminary and its illegitimate reach into certification. If clergy have a base, the powers of both congregation and seminary also become more legitimate in the long term. By the very dialogue with professional reality, their status could increase. Denominations could lay the foundation for these covenants. The way we do it now, with each "man" on his own, is no fun. I have yet to meet a man in one of the larger, potentially more secure parishes of Mayflower fame who is not in some kind of fight over his "package." If he is satisfied, you can bet some congregants are not and vice versa.

My strategy for security has been to deepen the contradiction, to confess the ambivalence, to tell my people when they ask about money how uneasy I am if I ask them for more. I give them the whole treatise on upward and downward mobility, the Mayflower issue, and maybe more than is written here. That confuses them good and proper. Usually I've gotten raises. I can imagine the time when that won't happen. I can certainly imagine the reasons.

As a woman with a husband who can somewhat support her, I write with trepidation. Single people may not have such securities. God knows a lot of congregations have starved ministers to death. For what we do, the going rate is ridiculous. The great majority of clergy, particularly those who retired before pension boards were as effective as they are now, are severely underpaid. Most lay people have so few people they can boss around that they love to boss pastors around. They have come to love the going rate. These attitudes really hurt; they violate the covenant we have signed on to defend.

To protect that covenant we have to break the Mayflower rules and take the risk that possibly our people will break them, too. Better to break the Mayflower rules in association than out of it.

CHAPTER 6

Taking the Measure of the River

There is an eleventh commandment in the ministry and that is, don't split the church. Its theology is the idolatry of unity. As one of the editors of a partisan newsletter at my church's general synod last year, I was berated for not writing a unifying article the second the issue we had been fighting for was defeated. *Thou shalt not schism, and if you do, we will punish you* was the message. Unity is so dear to the hearts of most church people that the very scent of conflict sends them all scurrying to their higher principles, the highest at the moment being some sort of tolerance and mutual acceptance no matter how idiotically the other is behaving. Don't even intrude on the discussion with matters of justice or truth; leave the Holy Spirit out of the discussion. What matters is that we get along.

Oddly, many people, men and women, think that their security is found in the avoidance of conflict. It is not, but that doesn't stop the unity people from having their say. Despite frequent chafing at the imperialism of the unity people, I do think there are a few places where conflict is inappropriate. Natural functions should not be disturbed, like eating, sleeping, drinking. There is no point in taking on the chair of your board of trustees at the church supper. You should definitely wait until dessert is finished. There is no point picking fights by yourself; all fights are worth a constituency, and if you can't get a constituency, that means there is no fight. All you have is your irritation; certainly you have no power or position or community from which to differ.

In the church we should be glad at the arrival of conflict. Glad. What conflict means is that we are about to get to know each other better, to know ourselves better, and to know our God better. We are about to connect. Conflict is the troubling of the water that brings the holier spirits into our midst. I question what's holy about unity because unity smoothes over our identities and makes God too easy to get along with, so easy in fact that I fear we are not getting to God through harmony at all, but rather to one of those famous idols whose legion names are safety. Soldiers find God while stuck in foxholes; I'm not sure clergy do. People tolerate those who "get along well" with other people; they are led, however, by people who willingly, happily, and consistently trouble the waters. Remember high school and the glee on people's faces when they would say, "She don't take no ____."

Conflict is the road to the crucifixion, and crucifixion is the road to resurrection. (I hope that reminds you of one of your sermons.) A good strategy for ministry is to deepen the contradictions between God and mammon. Deepening that contradiction will point people to the marvels inside them and out to the God who embraces those marvels.

Too many people are playacting. Lately it has become quite fashionable to act as though women's liberation were achieved. We "love" our jobs, our house, our spouse, our kids. There are no problems that can't be solved by improved communication or some such. But clergy know the function of such myths; we know how miserable too many people are. We know how unfinished God's work is. Thus we should be glad when people unwrap their turmoil and take the blanket of illusion off it.

More important, we should be glad for the projections that get lay people going after us. What better chance do we have for the unveiling, for the beginning of the process of recognizing our alienation so that it might be healed? Certainly not every time one of our people screams at us on the way out of church is a projection of their own inner turmoil. We may in fact have just preached a lousy, insulting sermon. But many times something more complicated is going on. We have pushed a button under which lies pain. Going after pain and finding its sources is absolutely necessary to the process of liberation. And there is nothing wrong with our having a lousy Sunday afternoon trying, with help if we can get it, to discover why we were as insulting as we were, if that's what it was. Trouble is the best university in the country; we should all go there and get our Ph.D.s.

On my first solo flight, in my first "senior" pastorate, I got into a real *brouhaha* almost on time at the beginning of my second year, the end of the honeymoon. Terror was the least of my feelings. The chair of the stewardship campaign was also a dean of a graduate department at the local university. For years he had been writing the stewardship letter himself and doing the whole campaign by himself. The letter was a horror movie, declaring the imminent demise

of the congregation should pockets not be deeply touched. One of
the other members said that she really thought something should
be done about this annual routine. If this were happening now, I
would work with her to do something about it. But back then I
hadn't found all the limits on my own responsibilities. Thus I
obliquely suggested to the stewardship chair that perhaps he would
enjoy a committee. As he jumped off his chair, stormed around the
room, and penned a letter of resignation to both the stewardship
campaign and the congregation, taking with him his large personal
annual pledge, which he took no time in revealing to me, I pon-
dered other careers. Perhaps I could be a missionary somewhere.
My overreaction was sublime. It still gives me a place to go when
these sorts of things repeat themselves, which they do. I just go to
my overreaction that day and sit and wait out the conflict, wait for
the mess to reach its high tide and then watch it wax and wane till
it is finished. (I also put a note on my calendar to visit the princi-
pals every three months until reconciliation or closure is reached.
Once conflict has peaked, I think it is time to reintroduce
harmony.)

My overreaction (o.r.'s I now call them for short) to this situation
developed as follows. I called a meeting of half the leadership of
the congregation and because they too found the situation uncomfortable, they all showed up. Then and there the agreement was
made that it had probably been the "right" thing to do and what a
shame, etc. That year's pledge campaign raised a tidy sum more
than the previous year had. People paid for the mistake of letting
one person have so much power for so long.

The good part of this o.r. was that we took the measure of the
river. We found out if we were going to be able to make our passage or not. The way we did it was by checking with each other.

The lesson is simple. Theologically, we all understand how you
can't wear the crown if you can't bear the cross. Experientially, we
have a ways to go. If we were to evaluate the conflicts we have
been in, both the large and the small, we would discover how good
they have been for us. How nothing else redistributes power so ef-
fectively as conflict and how redistributing power in organizations is
healthy. The more frequently it is done, the more open the organization. The more open the organization, the more possible it is for
people to find God there. The more closed, the more quiet, the
more concentrated and immovable the power, the less access there
is to the liberating movements of the Holy Spirit. These are the reasons we should be glad at the arrival of conflict.

Conflict is a bit different for women than it is for men. There is
the commandment to unify which everyone suffers from. I observe

that men overreact neither more nor less than women. For women there is also the commandment to pacify. Mothers and wives have staked out this role for themselves over the years and these family roles bleed into church behavior. We try to make everything right as a way of defending our gender. We look unwomanly if we are deepening contradictions and delighting in conflict. Someone is apt to attack our sexuality, to remember the coldness in their own mother which they could not abide and attach that coldness to us if we jump over the pacifying, unifying fence of Egypt. These attacks are not pleasant especially if we are making the mistake of locating our sexuality in pacification processes.

Has anyone seen my femininity? I seem to have misplaced it! Once again the choice is clear: Be insecure doing the job of ministry, leading unwilling people to and through cross and crown; or avoid conflict, play the unity game, pacify all parties, and hang out in Egypt till the conflicts there boil up uninvited and cause you and yours trouble because you don't know their names. There is more than one way to be insecure. There is more control in anticipating conflict, and some people say control gives them security. It can also, if too richly indulged, end up being unity's idolatrous sister and plunk you right back where you started—scared, behind the fence, looking for a ditch, surfacing only to pull strings and manipulate events. Best to know the measure of the waters and become expert at taking those measures and let the others fight it out. Neither our sexuality nor our security is in our power to pacify. Rather, both are found in our ability fully, richly, with sparks flying, to connect.

CHAPTER 7

The Security of Frequently Being Wrong

It is better to keep your mouth shut and appear stupid than to open it and remove all doubt.

Mark Twain

My security is at least my well tutored capacity to be wrong. My acquaintance with this capacity began as I and the secretary played the numbers game in the hyperactive campus ministry office where I did my internship. There, in the early seventies, things were so crazy so frequently that we needed mechanisms to defend ourselves. We came up with the number five. That was the number of strange things required to happen before we would declare a crisis or even a bad day. Five crises were considered normal; at the sixth, we could begin our various laments.

Thus the first student who was leaving school that morning in a huff was number one. That his parents were blaming the counseling service in the chaplain's office was only one and one-half. If the president's office called again about the gay rights group that appeared to be meeting in the chapel social room and how sinners of this stripe were uninvited on chapel grounds, that could be considered number two. If it was true that the chapel student newspaper did publish a picture of the dean in a sexual position with a baseball bat, that could be three and might qualify as four, too. Number five was usually a breakdown in equipment, inviting a round of complaints regarding how little money we had and how much work we had to do. That complaint had a way of getting philosophical and pretty soon you could declare the whole day problematic, no matter the time, and continue into a state of crisis. The numbers game made it legitimate.

Since that heady time, I have worked in many offices. Very few days have not required some version of the numbers game. Ministry is a constant, perpetual, unceasing set of interruptions of what others consider work. I can't remember a newsletter that actually got out on time. There is always a pastoral perplexity right ahead of its deadline.

One Christmas week we were dealing with a particularly high level of deadline anxiety regarding the two bulletins and sermons that needed to get done by Wednesday or some such, and it was as though someone had put up the free milk and cookies sign at the Congregational Church. Everyone was showing up, almost on purpose, as though it were a test of my ability to be a minister while getting some "work" done. Internally, the day was one of prayer: *Okay, God, you do want the secretaries furious at me for the rest of my life? Okay, God, I know this is your idea of a joke but I don't like making a fool of myself in front of hundreds of people, could you please get these people out of here?* But the children have no Christmas gifts, and my husband beat my daughter last night, and I can't stand the idea of getting on that plane and going to see my mother, and M. is drunk again and if she thinks I'm eating another of those dinners she prepares while drunk, she has another think coming. One is the count between prayers. Then two, etc. You can use numbers to get through a blood test when the needle is sticking in your arm, and you can use numbers to count curve balls that God throws at you, and you can use numbers to count the number of crises you can bear with no Christmas sermon or bulletin prepared. The numbers don't do anything magic; they just remind you every now and then that you are human and that you have limits.

The numbers lead me to the security of frequently being wrong. I have decided it is important to be wrong at least five times a week. Pick a number, any number. Make it your goal; try to meet it. Work at it if you must. It is actually quite amazing the number of times it is possible to be wrong in a given week. Given the chaos of ministry—and I know few for whom it is not chaos, whether Christmas chaos or campus chaos or just the Spirit's bubbles rising up in the congregation—it would be absurd to think that we could do very much right. So few of us ever get our long-range plan written, so urgent are the short-range tasks. So few of us work from a job description, how would we know if we were doing something right or wrong? Call on Mrs. T. or Mrs. B. this afternoon? Give thirty minutes to the desperate nonmember or the chair of your board of trustees? There are only thirty minutes and both want them. Build institutions and suffer the accusation the Samaritan escaped or escape with the Samaritan and watch the institution crumble and the task of caring for everybody fall to you solely?

It's both/and, most feminists will tell you. That is also the reason they work, on the average, 16-hour days. Men are also terrible workaholics; both overdo it.

There is security in being human. There is enormous security in knowing how frequently you are going to be wrong. Overextension is only one of the reasons why you will foul up. Others are fear, faithlessness, and stupidity. I once, mistakenly, gave a eulogy that exposed a family secret to three hundred people. I once believed a board of deacons who was lying to me about a certain mission commitment. I so much wanted to believe them that I just did. My mission people didn't take long to tell me what a sap I was. I have frequently and consistently overworked myself rather than trusting a process or problem to people in my congregation. I don't like to float down rivers; I like to steer down rivers. It's just easier to do things myself; it also has the distinct advantage of maintaining my sense of superiority over the congregation. My greater intimacy with godliness than theirs. My little game of being God.

I have avoided nursing homes for months after seeing some particularly frightening octogenarian who reminded me too much of where I was heading. I didn't tell anyone of the fear; I just stopped going for awhile. You can get away with that sort of thing. Many of us cheat our student interns, so easy is it to get away with leaning on them rather than mentoring them. In fact, it may be the very freedom we have as ministers that allows us to err so skillfully.

The problem for women with regard to error is that we always have sexism to lean on. In addition to the chaos and the fear, we can blame our pioneering status or the roadblocks of men. The existence of sexism doesn't mean we are never wrong; it just disguises our foibles. The problem for men with regard to error is that they've been trained to think of themselves as more closely linked to perfection than the other gender. Thus error is a bit harder to bear.

It probably doesn't matter too much who has more difficulty in sustaining and learning from errors. What matters is how frequently we are going to make them and how much security we could enjoy if, after predicting them, we could evaluate them.

There is probably nothing of more value in a congregation than the capacity to ask questions. What did you think of that meeting? How did you think I handled Mrs. J. when she attacked me? Often, people will say that they didn't see the attack, that Mrs. J. is just like that. Then we get to figure out what is making us so vulnerable to Mrs. J. Questions that assume critical capacity, to give and to take, give the numbers game sacramental status. They witness forgiveness, that cleansing moment that follows being wrong. It too is predictable.

CHAPTER 8

The Sacrament of the Calendar

Being busy does not make us secure, but you won't discover this unpleasant truth by observing clergy. Clergy, the great proponents of grace, stuff time with work. I knew a pastor who did not sup at the holy table of the calendar and he was despised. In addition to performing his ministerial duties, he was a poet. He wrote poems instead of attending three committee meetings a day while bearing a full counseling load and keeping the trustees out of trouble. His colleagues considered him a fugitive, a miscreant, a bit of a criminal. He did not follow the rules to work hard and long. Instead he preached sermons and performed sacraments and wrote poems. The very gall.

There is no more absurd moment than that which tries to conclude a clergy meeting. The better chairs allow for at least ten minutes for the performance of the ritual of setting the next meeting. Everyone, with deep sighs, has to explain at least once why he or she can't make a proposed date. The object of the interchange is to let everyone else know how busy you are, how needed you are, how deeply in demand you are, but how, nevertheless, with all that obligation pulling on your coat, you will show up once again for whatever we did today, good colleague that you are. Usually, someone will say that we can't get everyone or that they just have to go along without them. A vigorous negative will be declared to such a lack of inclusiveness, and the ritual will end with ink on paper marking time, a perfectly Protestant process.

Clergy get hooked on helping. We like to think that we can help a lot of people and thus set out to do so. We don't like to think that all this helping has to do with helping ourselves, filling the dry well that is sending us to God in the first place. That would be embarrassing. But most of us know the real limits on help: the limits on help itself, the limits on what we could do to help if help helped, the blazing error of trying to centralize help in a minister when everyone knows it has to be distributed through a congregation. We know fatigue and we know chaos and we know how deeply both affect our wisdom in any given situation. We know how they work to disqualify much of our caring, turning it into a commodity and away from a gift.

As commodity, help gives with one hand and sticks its other hand out for payment. The payment may be approval or intimacy, with us enjoying the power role, or it may be scoring points with a congregation who is as dizzy as we are with the notion of help. But the payment is never enough. Being busy with good things won't fill up our empty wells. The water of God is not for sale. Advocacy produces neither security nor salvation.

For women this hyperactivity of late Protestantism is a serious issue. We get to the table in the first place by inferring that we can at least be equal to men, if not their betters. So, we'd better perform, right? We had better make sure our date books are as full as their date books. It's an interesting fallacy for both practical and theological reasons.

First, women simply don't have the time to do ministry men's way. (Yes, there is a men's way; the fact that some men choose to be poets does not deny that there is a men's way of doing business.) Women do not have wives. Not having a wife is a major impediment to doing ministry men's way. We work a second shift. When we get home, we cook, mail birthday packages to the in-laws (usually both sets), and look for our children's lost dinosaurs. Unless we are single, we simply do not and cannot maintain the schedules men have maintained in ministry. If single, there is the matter of justice.

There is a trickier reason to wiggle out of the busyness box, and it is less lofty. We are destroying the profession, making it one where only the foolish dare apply. Even labor unions have achieved an 8-hour day; the idea that ministers would disavow leisure or art on behalf of work, as though we were better than the rest of the population, has an insidious effect on our congregations. Besides making it nearly impossible for them to accept the Gospel, because its chief proponent is denying it all week long, our workaholism separates us and disempowers them. God gets equated with the idea of work. The invitation to grace is not genuine.

There is another reason not to work so bloody hard at ministry, and it's personal. I need margin. I need down time. I need to be useless. I am not a ministry machine. Most of my friends say things like this to me all the time. I know I am not alone in the deep awareness of how my empty well won't fill by working it full.

So the practical shakes hands with the theological. God is not mocked or manipulated. The idea that hard work brings us or our people closer to God is idolatrous. Yes, effort is required, but the focus should be our journey towards God. Sometimes that journey may take work. Other times it may take rest. Sometimes we will be commanded to rest in our work, to not labor so laboriously. Other times to work in our rest, to battle with angels unaware. Whatever we can do to meet God on the two-way street, and let all our striving cease, will be good.

One caveat is in order. This process is not the same as laziness, nor is it the faking of being busy which is widespread among us. So brutal are the laws to be busy that many clergy act busy as a way of conforming, but aren't really busy at all. Rest takes an intention; the intention may be no larger than to goof off on behalf of God, but that is different than saying you are going to do a lot of things and then just not doing them. Fraud doesn't help ministry either.

Can you hold a job in late Protestantism living by grace and not by works? That is the question. I'm not sure you can, short of the Reformation that is coming or the association that is needed. But most of us, men and women, weren't just looking for a job anyway. We are willing to endure more than the usual religious stress precisely to obtain at least the usual religious security.

CHAPTER 9

The Decline of the Idols

Like so many other places where we seek security and do not
find it, the calendar betrays. The busy face of the late great Protestant work ethic is about to do us in. It makes a joke of our denominational commitments to family life, to lay empowerment, and to
grace. There is a heavy and interlocking set of penalties for what
appears at first to be the peccadillo of trying too hard. To comprehend the threat of the calendar and the imperialism of its clock, we
have to understand the origin of our busyness.

Many justify our overwork by the theory of decline. The Protestant churches are dying. Did you sign up to be the last generation
of Protestant clergy? Too few of us want to go to our fate with that
on our head.

I have wondered for years whether the old girls should survive.
(By the referent "girls" here to denominations, I mean something
universal which does not exclude the old "boys.") Perhaps women
have less investment in the old structures; we should have less, I
think, but that's another matter. Using the tried-but-true theory of
letting go of what you would really like to have, perhaps we could
just let them die and see if they have something to offer from the
edge of their graves. Saving nineteenth-century configurations
hardly strikes me as something worth dying for; I'm pretty sure that
when Jesus modeled crucifixion, institutions were not supposed to
follow suit. Even so, many of us are exerting ourselves to avoid
their decline and demise, as though preventing that would offer security.

We seem to enjoy tsk, tsking about the theory of decline of the
church. It allows all sorts of desperate bobbings in the water. It permits clergy to become more professional, as though increasing our
status would give us the good feelings of security. We have changed
our degrees around: master's is now insufficient; substitute doctor-

ate. We have indulged countless workshops and post-graduate train-
ings. The Clinical Pastoral Education movement came along just in
time to give us the patina of psychology. More recently, the various
management-by-objectives and derivatives have polished us even
further. We begin to be able to hold our heads up in the certified
and certifiable world.

These polishings, many of which are necessary to educate us
after the serious, but humorous, attempts that seminaries make,
don't provide an alternative to the theory of decline. They help us
do the job because extracurricular education is so much better than
the curricular ones we are provided these days. Ex ecclesia is
where the fun is. But having affirmed these polishings, one must go
on to ask their origins. They too shore up the collapsing sand
dunes of late Protestantism. They try to prevent erosion by bringing
us more into the professional framework of doctors, lawyers, and
electricians, each of which has more status currently than we do.
But to find true security, to see a significant renewal of the church
would require a fast exit from these frameworks, a crucifixion if
you will.

One of my more embarrassing professional experiences I call
the big nurse blues. There were about a dozen beds in the intensive care unit. which was built in a semi-circle with two entrances.
The person I was visiting had been there for over a month and was
in room 11, just inside the north entrance. In bed 12 there was a
person in the last throes of death. A code blue had been called and
about a dozen people and all sorts of machinery were surrounding
her bed. I was not unmoved by all this nor was I involved. I simply
entered behind the crowd, went straight to room 11, and there engaged my person in something resembling conversation, because
he too was in the final stages of a devastating cancer. He was aware
of what was going on next door and had more reason than I to see
its horror. The head nurse on the unit, who I knew from many
other visits there, left her post at the code blue bed, came over to
me, and in front of my patient, lambasted me. *How dare you walk
through a code blue? How dare you interrupt our important work?
Are you not prepared in seminary for these protocols? Who trains
you clergy anyway? The lot of you, the pack of you,* she hissed out,
*are the stupidest, dumbest, blankety blankety blank group I have
ever seen.*

When we talked about it later, because that day there was no
talking, she told me that she was at the end of a 16-hour shift. She
told me that she had been observing clergy in the intensive care
ward for about a dozen years. She told me horror story after horror
story about clergy making 30-second visits, of clergy being absurdly

useless during code blues, of people taking powders when they were really needed. She had stored up a lot of anger, and my just walking by that day had pushed her over the top. No, I do not think this had anything to do with my being female. This had to do with a mountain of incompetence, and I just happened to be the last one to climb up. She felt that I or someone should have seen how needy she was, how much she needed someone to stand next to her during this particular, very difficult death. Someone should have known how much she put into this patient, how this patient had no relatives. Someone should have cared. She got to make this public, historical accusation at me.

Becoming more professional will not hurdle this accusation. Doing more work on death and sickness might. But a more basic matter is at stake and she knew it. It had to do with our capacity to care and not with our training or skill. Skill enables care; skill is not care. We are generalists in a world of specialists. The world needs us that way, needs our eyes as expert as possible so that we can see looks on faces, so that we can have a finely hewn sense of when to help big nurse and when to leave her alone, that we can have protocols and know when not to be threatened by protocols. I don't begin to claim to have these gifts and graces.

But I know we won't get them by the defensiveness of getting more and better training. I know we won't get to them if we keep working so hard that we burst through the corridors of death on our way to "finishing" our calling for the day so that we can get home and do some more work. Working better or working faster won't solve the problems that churches in decline are facing.

The pretentious posture of overload is sapping the church of its life. Its anxiety is an insult to the Spirit and to everything that is holy. Big nurse is holy; her anger that we are not there for her is holy. Our calendars are not.

The church is stuffed. It has indigestion. The point is not "how to learn how to say no." Rather it is to learn to say more _no_ to anxious hustle and bustle and more _yes_ to the graces of God's good life.

Prophetic types may be the worst offenders. It doesn't seem to have occurred to us that there is an entire culture, economy, and political system working against us. These systems have a lot of secretaries who type well, xerox machines that work, and access to advertising that makes our posters and flyers and brochures look smaller than the stone that David threw at Goliath. We underestimate both the strength of the opposition and the size of our alternative. We are a biblical people and when people meet us, something about our uniqueness ought to show. Big nurse was screaming at me because nothing unique showed. I glided as rapidly through pain as any other professional on her floor.

What ought to show in us is not our credentials, but rather a firm trust that the small is more important than the large and that eventually the small will overpower the large. From that perspective denominations deeply in decline are matters of hope, simply waiting for a few generalists to strip off the dead outer layers and find the new growth.

Neither the massive energy of overwork nor the one hundredth workshop will accomplish these delicate tasks. God's timetable doesn't fit on my calendar's pages. I get my piece of it and I have to count on you getting and doing yours.

There's nothing virtuous about massive energy unless you are an atom bomb. There's nothing evil about getting a good night's sleep. Putting what you can eat on your plate rather than stuffing yourself is good manners.

Deep in decline, we do have tasks. Strip off the old skin. Enjoy the new growth. Wait on the Lord and renew our strength.

CHAPTER 10

Peace Burps:
The Permanence of Insecurity

Every Sunday in my parish, right before the sermon, we sing hymn number 524: *Lead Me, Lord.* It goes, "Lead me Lord, Lead me in thy righteousness; make my way plain; for it is Thou, Lord, Thou, Lord only, who makest me dwell in safety." If I can stop rehearsing long enough, this is the most worshipful part of the service for me. Most of us know that safety is impossible, and yet we seek it all the time. In that gap, that hope that there is a God who will do what we know cannot be done, religious faith abounds, bouncing between fantasy and reality, causing us to feel permanently embarrassed at how dearly we covet what we cannot achieve. Or more precisely, how dearly we covet what we can only have by letting go of it. These are the conundrums of God.

Perhaps for some ministers the repeated singing of the hymn sinks in. Maybe they are able to stop searching for safety in all the wrong places. Or maybe God's safety isn't even safe.

Or at least that is what I have come to conclude. In ministry safety is divine. It is certainly not professional. What with the sexism inside us and the sexism outside us, the risks inherent in divine obligations (men, too, run up against the rigors of call), and our own refusal to stop rehearsing, it better be God who guarantees safety because no one else is.

Take a silly example. If a woman offers to take the minutes at a church meeting, a complication ensues. Later, she may feel that she shouldn't have volunteered. How typically womanly of her! Men may feel uneasy, wondering if she is collecting ammunition for a later attack. Both are likely to feel guilty that their association has not been more liberated. Talking about it only makes the exquisiteness of the complication more certain. We are supposed to be leaning towards the coming time of God and what are we doing but spending hours on the minutes? The trivial has a way of taming ambition while interfering with mission.

Those who feel permanently caught in the petty do not feel too good about themselves. And a lack of that confidence, that spark, that tipping of the balance towards the positive breaks many a meeting. There are vibrations, and they matter. There is spirit, and it is the key to every meeting. Putting men and women together in professional roles rarely produces positive sparks. Women are so new at it, we frequently get mired in the petty. (I've been at it for eighteen years, but that doesn't prevent a 28-year-old man from being more comfortable in meetings than I am.)

We should all be better than this. But we are not. Men are simply unaware of the antennae women have out all the time. Very few are interested enough in how we are or what we think. They may miss the significance of the minutes being taken by a woman again, but most women will not. Some women may overlook it because they have made a decision to lop off the uneven edges of this transition towards androgyny in the ministry. People do lop off the edges. It helps them sail into the smoother water of security. They do it because trusting others to be your friend is so much harder than being friendless. Smooth edges simply feel more comfortable than rough ones.

Repression seems like such a good idea. When I have tried it, however, the short-term benefits have always competed with the long-term ones. When I am able to convince myself that I really don't feel as uncomfortable about something as I seem to, I manage to find some peace. But it is a peace that burps. My discomfort comes back up on me. I may swallow a female colleague's eagerness to take the minutes, make the phone calls, and clean up the coffee only to put her down in some obnoxious way later on. I also will antagonize my colleagues who perpetuate this practice.

Given what I know about sexism and its depth, I worry when things are going well. Men are taking minutes, serving coffee, volunteering to do work after meetings instead of assigning work during meetings. Maybe they even are sharing a feeling or two. I get nervous. I'm so good at predicting insecurity that it has become my friend. At least I get to be right about something.

Of course, there's nothing wrong with a little healthy suspicion. Smooth waters may mean that you're drifting. The men may be following instructions rather than being liberated. They too can float along, avoiding the rough spots. But if you're drifting, eventually some stray sexism may run you aground. You may discover that men you thought were friends, the ones you had pacified so thoroughly (by perhaps taking good minutes), don't really know what it means to be your friend. The men who pacified us in our raging feminist stage may also run aground on our rejection of their friendship. True friendship is a haven of security; it is godlike. That so many of us have so few genuine friends demonstrates the depth of our insecurity.

Friendship requires that the waters be tested frequently and thoroughly. A friend will swim through the pettiness of the minutes with us. Some good rough bumps guarantee the friendship in a way that sailing around the bumps never will. Yet I meet more clergy, both men and women, who have been disillusioned by friends rather than confirmed by them.

The fear of being the victim of sexism plagues our attempts to build the friendship. Women, in our inability to unhook from men, are (don't you love faddish phrases?) co-dependent with men in sexism. We need it as much as they do. Can you imagine having to change our own tires? Or having to meet our own God? It's a good thing we have men to kick around a little longer.

Not that God is slowing down the timetable of liberation. All sorts of women have pinched their noses and jumped into the waters. We have joined South Africans and Nicaraguans and Chinese and Filipinos and African Americans and millions of others in tasting what it's like to desire safety and at the same time require freedom. Paradox is no longer a stranger to us.

Already we have done all sorts of things we never thought we could. I have actually counseled two paraplegics who were getting married about how to have sex. They acted like they thought I knew what I was doing. They did not know that I was praying urgently without ceasing. I have counseled men who accepted my authority as their pastor in a way that even I did not. I have buried, married, and baptized and, almost every time, have been a bit amused that the world allowed me, a mere female, to do such a thing.

Like many women, I still think that something will come in the mail saying that there has been a mistake and that, in fact, I am not ordained. I don't worry that my baptism will be rendered null and void or that my status as a child of God will be changed. In those matters I am secure. It's this business of being on the road to freedom. . .and thinking that God sent me there, that scares me. Imagine, women being allowed to use the holy words, touch the holy symbols, keep the holy spaces holy, or being close enough to the name of God to be able to take that name in vain. Imagine the magnificent inappropriateness of it all. It is just as scary to turn around and head back for Egypt as it is to keep going. Turning around would be the coward's way, the faithless way, the way that would deny God God's fun. Plus returning would cause burping. Going forward is going to mean hassling about the minutes or some other crazy thing and living most of the time with most people mad at you for not being satisfied with the way things are. Satisfaction trivializes God's plans for us. And there you have the double bind, the uneasy pact that freedom makes with security. It is a complete circle.

There are a whole list of places you can't go to find safety. Not adjustment. Not liberation. Not forward and not backward. Not higher salaries or status; not in repression or studiously, loudly avoiding repression. Not in hard work nor in staying permanently busy with good works. Not in any idolatry whatsover. We may have to acknowledge the permanence of stress and lean only on God. Just as number 524 tells us to.

CHAPTER 11

Dwelling Among Our Own People

The Shunammite woman gave Elisha, the holy man, hospitality. He wanted to pay her back. She was offended by the very idea. "I dwell among my own people," she said.

Whenever any one of us can say these words, we are secure. If the words cannot come to us, we are not secure.

I thought of this when a woman sounding much too young called to say that she wanted her daughter baptized. Of course we could baptize her daughter. But did the mother know what it meant to baptize a daughter? Of course not, my cynicism told me. The church may no longer be able to afford the expense of our baptismal theology, but at least we can try. I explained to her that baptism gave her daughter back to God and that our congregation stood in for God during the child's life. We became her people. That meant some very simple things like participation in our church, raising the child among us, risking being enough a part of us that she would weep at our funerals just as we would weep at hers. She didn't want all that, she said. She just wanted her daughter baptized. Well, there is no such thing as just baptized. Baptism is dwelling among a people. You can't just get sprinkled and leave.

I understand that many who are baptized will go on to live in other worlds and to weep at other funerals than those we have here. That doesn't prohibit a person from being part of a people. But so many of us now prefer a sprinkling to a baptism, a network to a community. We prefer being a *person* to being a *people*.

God spoke the great words of covenant to the Hebrew people and to us: *I will be your God and you will be my people.* These words surround us with security; they bathe us in safety. If we have a God and if we have a people, what else do we need?

You'll find the root of all major social problems in the rubble of the breakdown of community. Our failure to care for our environment means, fundamentally, that we want our slice and don't care if future generations or developing countries get theirs. Let's take all the natural resources and spend them on ourselves. Let's use up all the topsoil now. We are not a people and we have no God. The ridiculous risks we have taken in developing nuclear weaponry shout the same message. We are so important and we have so many enemies that we and our enemies can justify the absurdity of mutually-assured destruction. We are not a people and we have no God. The atrocities of race and class and gender, which divide up communities into rigid hierarchies, grow out of broken community, too. Blacks and whites, rich and poor, male and female, we are not a people and we have no mutual God.

When we hear the Shunammite woman declare herself part of a community, we listen in with jealous ears. We too would like to tell the holy men that we don't need anything from them. But we do need; in fact, our need is desperate. Private community does not erase the need for public community. But private community is a necessary stop on the way to the larger configurations.

We need to know people well enough so that they'll be honest and real with us. Recently, I sat at a summer's eve dinner table joined by friends of nearly twenty years' duration. Right in the middle of the food, I got ridiculously sentimental. I remembered the college days that brought us together, the times when they told me they didn't like what I was doing, and I told them I didn't like what they were doing. Oh, those times of deep honesty are very few. Mostly we get through our dinners without very deep sentiment. We joke about each other's clothes, but not about the way we are living.

What it means to have good friends is so good, it is almost unspeakable. We remember details of each other's weddings. Children's baptisms. Talking on the phone while she was in labor with their second child and on the way to the hospital. Meeting at motels in places like Scranton, wherever that is. There is a kind of security in dwelling among a people that is as close to the sublime as I plan on getting this side of the Jordan. The security depends on trusting your friend to wade in the muddy parts as well as the clear ones. The security doesn't take away the stress; it only assures us that we are not in the mud alone.

My richest experience in human community reminds me of that summer-time dinner party. It is the oneness I feel with that group of women ministers whom everyone is doing a research paper on. We are the pioneer generation, the first ones, the ones whom the younger ones now think are a bit obnoxious. You should hear women in seminary talk about women who were pioneers. They are convinced that we are too serious, too angry, too bruised by all the early doors that slammed in our faces to be a part of their people. Younger women are convinced that they are going to have it easier than we in the ministry, and they are right. But what they do not know yet is that the young are integrally a part of the old; they exist to show us what was foolish in our ways. The species advances through this tension; why shouldn't women and clergy use the same push and pull to find their way down the road?

What amazes me about this struggling community of pioneer women is how little we knew what we were doing. We did not know that we were surveying new land. We didn't know we were pioneers till most of the pioneering was done. But whenever we gathered, there was a kind of unbeatable, immeasurable bliss. Somebody understood what we just said. Click. Nobody singled us out as wierd or different or shook our hand and said, _wow, I never met one of you before._ The game of zoo was suspended.

Community marches forward unawares, I think. When we dwell among our own people, we can trust the other to tell us when we are wrong. We also can experience a bit of bliss, the wonder of not having to explain ourselves because everybody else understands why in this family we put ketchup on the eggs. No one remarks on our strangeness because it is not strange to them. Community also guarantees conflict: the young are expected to differ from the old and to do so vigorously. If that means they must put down the old, fine. It doesn't matter. But it does hurt. Still we are a part of the same people.

Community, the becoming of one people, could solve all the major social problems of our time. It could heal our very souls. Oddly, the public capacities of community often get overshadowed by its private capacities.

When we know we dwell among our own people, we are free to stand out ahead of them or over against them or separate from them. We can live alone if we are part of a people. We can prophesy if we are part of a people. We can dare to speak truth as part of a people because we can trust the other people to correct us if we are wrong.

The fact that community has all these advantages does not mean that it is not also a pain in the neck. There is something about being a "woman minister" that feels like a noose around the neck. Mess up and every other woman messes up with you. Succeed and every woman succeeds with you. It is very hard to find a place to be alone, to enjoy the same differentiated turf that men stand on by virtue of being men. If John makes a great discovery, John makes it. If Susan makes the great discovery, a woman scientist is lauded as having done well.

Families endure the same burden. One young man told me that the fact that everyone in his family is very cerebral, very intellectual, very much a good thinker is oppressive to him. He is not like that, but feels he must be or risk not being a part of his people. What gives us the strength to stand outside our own people, to be different? It is the quality of life within our communities. If everyone is forced to be cerebral, our community life is defensive, insecure, unsure. If, on the other hand, we can settle into a community where difference is anticipated, then out of that security will flow creativity, newness, the ability to stand outside the intimacy of it all without being cast out.

Congregations are a delightful source of community. And everyone who knows congregations knows that there are insiders and there are outsiders. At any given moment, there are some people who just can't abide what is going on. These people tend to change seats as ministers and other leaders in the church change. Those *in* with me might have been *out* with the previous pastor, and this musical chairs routine will continue when I am gone. I have come to believe that congregations need these ins and outs, that what makes for community is not good feeling all around, but people willing to stand for different parts of the shared Gospel, people willing to defend different ways of doing things and to stand outside the center for awhile.

When we baptize a child and say to him or her that we want them as a part of our community, we are not asking them to go with our flow. We are asking them to improve our flow over time. A community has high expectations for its members. We are not just looking for security when we dwell together. We are looking for the excellence to which God has called us as a people. If we get stuck in the security of being together, we'll circle the wagons and become defensive. We may literally consume each other. Breaks in the circle will keep that from happening; new people, new data, new ways are welcomed in communities that want a future. Newness gets drowned out in conformist, frightened communities, which unfortunately many of our congregations are.

In nurturing community, churches must be very careful. We do not grow if our circle is too tight, if newcomers quickly see that the current insiders have all the power and no intention of sharing their seats. We do grow, both numerically and spiritually, if power is constantly being redistributed, if people are changing seats and inviting each other to express differences.

Women who are clergy will make a better contribution to the ministry if they are able to hear the criticisms of younger women. Community will deepen our contribution in a way that nothing else

can. Our congregation will be richer for its quarrels. Our families
will be richer for our outcasts if the outcasts are willing to jump in
and mix it up every now and then, and if the resident family tyrant,
whoever it is, doesn't shoot them at the door.

When the Shunammite woman told Elisha that she didn't need
anything from him, she was wrong, as the story goes on to prove.
The fact that she dwelt among her own people was wonderful.
Good for her, we say, through our envy and our hope. But when the
outsider comes along, do what she did. Give him a room in your
house and let community flow and grow. As it flows and grows, it
will make us secure.

PART III

Power

CHAPTER 12

Excluded Hands Also Ordain:
An Introduction

Publicly, Protestant communions are bending over backwards to include women. We should be glad at this increasing recognition, but I rarely find one of us who is. We do not experience the inclusion that the press releases promise. Nor do we experience power. What we experience, and I think rightly so, is the creaking of an ancient heavy door, slowly opening, with some pulling it open and others pushing it closed. No one really knows yet if the door will open fully, so long has it been stuck closed, so enormous the effort will be to pry it free. Just this week I heard another story of a female dean of a prominent Protestant seminary who was given tenure by her faculty, but then asked to resign as dean. The male faculty voted against her and the females voted for her. Mind you now we're supposed to be beyond the historical ambivalence about women in positions of ecclesiastical power!

To some of us, this is a case of sour grapes. After all the effort, can it be possible that more is required? In the introduction, I said I wanted to understand that experience at the Tri-Boro Bridge where the truck took my lane and the policeman assisted the driver in doing so. I want to get underneath my terror at that man who shook his penis at me. I don't think it was just a traffic problem but rather a video of the audio that plays constantly in my mind: *Be careful, you're not safe here.*

Frequently, Roman Catholic women point the way to power and safety. They experience the resistance to women as priests so much more directly. Perhaps Catholic leadership (particularly that of Women's Ordination Now) can show us a way into the Protestant experience of power for women.

I should be glad for the 35,000 words, "Partners in the Mystery of Redemption," in which the Bishops declared sexism a sin and affirmed the priesthood of all males. I should rejoice that the church is moving some of its toes off mine. To boo Catholicism booing sexism is more sour grapes.

There are a lot of things I should do. As an ordained minister in the United Church of Christ, I know of my affiliation with Christ. I know I stand within his legacy. I know how holy the hands, even if all male, that touched my head and said I was to be like Jesus. I took that afternoon in Tucson, Arizona, very seriously, seriously enough to ask that one of the local Roman Catholic sisters be invited to lay hands on me with the rest of the men. I had panicked when I realized that all the hands were going to be male. My last-minute rearrangement was rejected by the Committee on the Ministry: No, Sister Rachel could not be a part of the laying on of hands. How about a nice Scripture reading, they said? No kidding. I should have fought that prohibition and exclusion right then and there. I didn't. There are a lot of things I should do. Now, when I remember my ordination, I am ashamed. Ashamed that I didn't fight for female hands. Ashamed that the church for so long kept ordained powers in the hands of men. Ashamed that the holiness that initiated me into this life was all male. Yes, Christ was present in the very historic, yet morally polluted, laying on of those hands. The grapes were already a bit sour right from the beginning. I was not altogether glad that day, even after the double rainbow appeared in the desert sky. Yes, it did.

Because of my commitment to Jesus, and through him to God, I should love better and longer; I should always forgive. I should prohibit the sun from setting on my anger. I should let go of the centuries of injustice against women and not be so uptight about maintaining my lane against intruders. My frequent failure to do so accustoms me to the disappointment of not being glad.

Maybe Jesus would have been happy if a drunk downed a fifth and no more or if a prostitute turned fewer tricks per week. Two steps forward, one step back is fairly normal for a spiritual journey. Jesus probably would have the wisdom to enjoy small reductions in the defense budget or fuller shelves in the food pantry. He talked an all-or-nothing line, I know, but when the chips were down, he accepted just about everybody and everything. He had a radical vocabulary and a liberal behavior. He therefore would tolerate the Bishops' backhanded compliment to women: that we should have expanded leadership roles at almost every level of the church except the priesthood.

I suppose the buck of justice stopped short of the priesthood for the same tired reasons. Jesus was a man and therefore the apostolic succession is male and therefore priests must be male. The grapes won't be good if men don't bless them. The succession will be violated. As though priests or ordained minsters, any of us, are capable of imitating Jesus.

Sorry. I know too many priests too well. They are as far away from being like Jesus as I am. The line of succession was gone a long time ago when the first priest sneaked a buck out of the collection plate or bedded the first nun or fellow priest. As I figure it, that was 2 A.D.

By the twelfth century the church had a great way of handling the sin of the priest. In a famous heresy decision, it said that the bread was good even if the priest wasn't. The grapes were good even if the priest wasn't. Doesn't that mean that the Mass bears its mysteries regardless of gender? Any priest who breaks bread and serves wine without inside knowledge of the violated Christ violates by that very act. If we don't know these things about ourselves, then surely our people know them about us. They are not fooled by apostolic succession; they tolerate most of what we say as quaint and disregard the rest. They eat the bread and drink the wine despite their knowledge of us, not because of it.

The fact that the Bishops' document stopped short of ordination for women violates the rest of what it says. Even if Jesus would have had the saintliness to be glad at the obvious breakthroughs, most will not. Most will see the sexism of binding the priesthood to specific genitalia. Many Roman Catholic women will bear another wound, unable to understand why the church they love so much has refused once again symbolic entry to its inner sanctum.

Few will be surprised. Everybody I know takes bets on when Catholics will ordain women. One hundred years is the standard answer or "one year after priests are permitted to marry." Maybe the church will get the message when the seminaries are empty and they are forced to permit women out of need. Just like Rosie the Riveter.

Organizations promoting the ordination of women actually are much more concerned about ministry than ordination anyway. Many women have already declared that they'd not want to be ordained to the same old priesthoood. I agree completely and deeply respect those Catholic women whose hands were prohibited from touching me.

In the Protestant church, I see our job as creating a new field and not merely sending women down to play with the boys. Our field will bring together agency and communion, the public and the private. Both men and women in ministry are needed for this task.

We Protestants demanded to have women ordained and that right early. It has only occurred to us in these later years, now that over half of the people in Protestant seminaries are women, that this extended priesthood solves little. Women have now proven that we are as good—and as bad—as men are at ministry. We have shown how little difference there really is between men and women in the pulpit. The Catholic Church will discover the same thing 100 years from now. Compared to ministry, women's ordination is no big deal. The big deal is how to get good grapes, able wounds, how to imitate a holy man. The big deal is how to find gladness after things are soured. The big deal is justice, even if two steps march forward and the third gets pushed back.

True power is not the power to be ordained. Power only begins as we get the modern Pharisees off our toes, as we gain the capacity to realize ecclesiastical justice for women and for men. Public power is so much more necessary than parochial power for women. (In fact, one could argue that women would not be ordained in significant numbers at all if it were not for the larger, simultaneous movement of feminism in society.) The ecclesiastical injuries only reflect the social injuries. I no longer fantasize about church leading society when the evidence is so strong that it happens the other way.

When husbands can no longer get away with beating their wives, justice for women will arrive. When women get the same dollar for their labor as men do, justice will arrive. When boys are raised to be like girls as well as girls being raised to have the privileges of boys, justice will arrive. When child care gets the fraction of the budget that now goes to killing, justice will arrive. These are the matters that require the attention of ordained women; these are the matters that Christ would care about first, not whether or not people of our gender can serve the sour grapes and broken bread. This hierarchy, not the "apostolic" one, has become most important to most women in ministry.

The reason women need power is that we need justice. We need justice so we can be safe. We need justice so that we have the space to develop our own authority.

I don't mean to trivialize the struggle for ordination, just to be clear that it is a secondary matter to the larger issue of justice for all women. We don't need to be stuck with sour grapes. We can and should change the focus of our anger and forgive not just the church for its sins against women, but the larger social order for its tangle of sexism. Power for women in ministry may begin with ordination, but that is by no means its final stop. By teaching me the hierarchy of justice, Sister Rachel's excluded hands ordained me as much, if not more, as those who thought they were Christ's official representatives that colorful day long ago in the desert. The lessons of exclusion are lessons in power. In the next chapter I tell what I know about open lanes to power for women in ministry.

CHAPTER 13

Opening Up New Lanes:
Repentance as Power

Women need power. We need to keep our lanes. There really is not a more attractive word for it than power. Without power we are condemned to our insecurities. Without power we are condemned to alienation. We can make no peace with either the size or the limits of our own authority. Without power we make promises that we can't keep. Without power we cannot heal the breach. If we can't heal the breach—that war between agency and communion, the battle open systems wage on closed systems—then we can't do our job. We need power to do our jobs. Keeping our lanes is about our egos, for sure, and it is about keeping our jobs. (Because I am white, I don't always see the parallels between women's need for power in a world men think of as their own and the needs of racial minorities for power. I just know the similarities are there. I am not implying here that only women's lanes are threatened.)

The power of strength won't really help us because (a) we don't have it biologically and (b) its use, even if we could get it, would only reinforce the false priority that values strength. Even bettering our opponents professionally is a bow at the altar of the old ways. Humiliating our opponents may feel like fun in old notions of how power games are played, but we will hurt ourselves more than them. Bitterness and cynicism turn in on us and make us brittle; we have already seen that in too many potential heroines. Women will find no lasting victory that way. Flo Kennedy said it best a long time ago: "What does it matter if it's a king or queen standing on top of the dung heap?" Nor can we borrow power in our continued intimacies with men. Even if they appear to be including us in their game by "sharing" power, we must be careful. Most of us really didn't want to play on the same old field, but on a transformed one.

Of course, women can and do have power in these masculine ways. There is nothing more moral about us. The question is whether we can realize our best selves, our most sophisticated communion, and find a way to get the power we need without taking it from men. The question is whether we can open new fields and new lanes, leading men into using our method of expanding the pie rather than cutting it up. With the power to heal the breach, we can transform the divisions into new ways of wholeness. We are after the capacity we need to keep our promises to God, to forgive our enemies, while not being pushed aside by them.

One strategy for getting power is repentance. We repent of our participation in the old ways; "they" repent of their participation in the old ways. We open up new lanes.

Once we are moving toward repentance, the methods of getting power are fairly clear. Nobody will give us power. Because we are finally standing on the solid ground of acting with and for rather than against, we are free from our own communal instincts to take power. We can say openly that we want it without fear that we are going to be cruel in the process. That doesn't mean that we won't make the mistake at times of acting against. We also know how to overdo agency.

To get power, we simply have to use and take power and act on behalf of the criteria we have stated. We care. We speak. We make jokes. We provide hospitality. We keep doing those things long after the opposition has flown its colors. Power is really born in the endurance more than in the debut.

We are most powerful, I think, when we require that the church and society repent of their sins against us as women while standing ready to forgive and receive the transformation that implies. In my ordination it was called "speaking the truth in love." I used to think that youth had only one struggle, that of forgiving itself for growing old. Now I see the same struggle toward maturity everywhere. We who build community and "adore the people" must hold those communities accountable, and ourselves within them, and move forward by the process of forgiveness.

Yes, it is wrong what church and society have done to women. It is wrong what we have allowed them to do to us. Yes, this must be said out loud. We are in on the game of abuse; we help other people abuse us. Yes, the days are long in which we must experience and understand this double knowledge. Gone is the moment when sophisticated communion can hold onto the feeble hope that women were just "victims." Yes, God will lend us the love to forgive the injuries, even the rapes, even the murder of wife by husband in a pandemonium of historical sexual permission, even the waste of our gifts on the highways. Yes, the streets will be restored to dwell in, the breaches will all be repaired.

To blame others only for our injury is a mistake. To blame ourselves only for our injury is a mistake. To resist the forgiveness that
comes to us for our participation, our silence, our sitting in the
stands for so very long, is a mistake. To assume that the mother and
father in God is too weak to forgive the sins of sexism is a mistake.
To waste time brooding over victims and the victim in us is a mistake. For now we have the simultaneous task of opening new lanes
while holding on to our own, the simultaneous task of judgment
and forgiveness, of mercy and anger, communion and agency. The
breach is enormous. Power in the ministry is living in that breach,
ever hopeful of its healing.

My power is my ability to forgive that truck driver while not letting him push me around. If he poisons me with anger against him,
he wins his lane. If I, in a fuzz of Christian tenderness masquerad-
ing as Christian love, "allow" him the lane, I lose the lane. Eventually my power as a justice maker is the opening of new lanes, the
making sure that he has a lane and that I have a lane, the realiza-
tion of the Gospel message of plenty in political and economic
terms. My power must learn to discern when I am holding too
fiercely to my own space or my own lane, when I internalize the
selfishness of the very systems that I oppose.

Even a simple metaphor like holding a lane reveals the many
dangers, the many places to get stuck on the way to transformation.
Soon we see that the process of personal power applies to larger
areas as well. Until and unless the United States admits wrong in
certain of its foreign policies that have been unjust to the people of
Vietnam or Nicaragua or El Salvador, it really will have no legitimate
power. All of its power will be only the prop of injustice, of force
wrongly used. It is bully power, the very kind the truck driver used
against me, bully power backed up by cop power, propped up by
expectations about women drivers or yellow people who are always
assumed to be in the wrong. Power wrongly used is frequently
propped up by sexism or racism or some macho combination.

Until the United States is able to forgive itself and others are
able to forgive it, the power will remain dependent on the props
and the force. A similar process of admitting wrong, experiencing
forgiveness, and getting on with the work of making justice must
happen if sexism is to be overcome.

Remarkably, the Soviet Union has shown us a bit of the way. It
may, of course, abort the process at any stage. Foreign Minister
Eduard A. Shevardnadze of the Soviet Union was quoted in the _New
York Times_ as saying, "We violated the norms of proper behavior.
We went against general human values. I am talking, of course,
about the dispatch of troops to Afghanistan. We committed the most

serious violations of our own legislation, our party and civilian norms."[1] An act of repentance of this magnitude is amazing. It shows that one is possible.

The beginning of the end of sexism will be in a mutual act of repentance of this size. It is possible. The power of women requires that we confidently expect these repentances and that we receive them when they come. They will not come through the newspapers, but rather in particular, personal, local work. The transformation that we seek will require an expertise in the power of forgiveness.

I know of no better way to develop that expertise than to develop congregational community. There the accountabilities are most clear, most personal, most touchable. The goal of power for women has as its objective justice in community, justice that begins with women's safety and authority being secured, but does not selfishly stop there. One of the great selfishnesses of our time is the way straight, middle-class, white women have understood sexism as their own little problem without understanding the double and triple jeopardies of other kinds of women—and men. Women, too, can get stuck in agency, in dividing ourselves from others and not being able to see beyond the end of our own noses. This is an aborted repentance.

Universal justice is possible, and women in ministry are one of the important streams leading in that direction. Congregations are our sites, the river banks within which we run. Congregations are a model, a place to learn how to forgive and how to transform. We are a good stream precisely because we have such good places to flow.

NOTE

1. Eduard Shevardnadze, "Quote of the Day," _The New York Times,_ 24 October 1989.

CHAPTER 14

Befriending Our Congregations

All of this complication does not mean that we are powerless.
We have plenty of power if we understand what power is and what
it is not. Powerlessness is the frustration of capacity, the wasting of a
person's gift. Power is realized capacity, the release of one's gifts
with the expressed purpose of releasing the gifts of others. It is the
ability to travel in your own lane without having to knock somebody else out of theirs. The theological assumption is that there are
plenty of lanes, that life and its goodies are abundant rather than
scarce. For women to do ministry does not mean that men cannot
or vice versa. It is only those people wed to the status quo of one-
lane highways, where everyone is condemned to move fast and furi-
ously, who don't understand this; they live with the illusion that
power is strength. But strength does get them most of the lanes and
much of what is known as "real" power. That one-lane society
where agency alone matters is not the place where (some) women
want to realize their capacities.

For most clergy the primary locus of power is the congregation,
or it should be. There we release our gifts and realize our capacities, among people who have called us to do that among them
while they themselves are doing the same thing. As nice as this
sounds, the fact is that most ministers don't really like their congregations. They think of them in various ways as idiots, objects of ma-
nipulation, barriers in their lane. Half of the clergy meetings and
workshops I attend are courses in how better to manipulate the laity toward our own ends.

Parker Palmer in an extended critique of objectification as the
problem with religious education tells of meeting with a group of
clergy who were sharing the frustrations of their work and the difficulty of finding personal support. One said, with an air of cer-

tainty, "Well, you can't expect to have your needs met by the people (read laity who are in some sense the *objects* of your efforts)." All the clergy present quickly agreed.[1]

The professionally distant attitude expressed here is a guaranteed way to frustrate the capacities of ministers. What I have experienced in my congregations is precisely the opposite of what this group was saying. My experience is that if you *do* depend on the members of your parish for a mutual support, if you *do* treat them as friends instead of objects, if you *do* expect to have your needs met by people in your parish, then a whole community of possibility opens up. Never having done it the other way—not out of design, but out of inability to do it the objective way—I don't know what happens the other way. Like many women I know, I am hopelessly, but creatively, mired in my own subjectivity.

What I observe in other congregations with "professional" ministers of this stripe is frustrated capacity, power struggles littering the one lane on which the fight is occurring, loneliness, and God's grace squeezed out. This is not a critique of professionalism for ministers. We are, I think, professionals by virtue of what we profess, which is the grace and love of God. I am not advocating a "low church" democracy or a "feel good" psychologization in which the minister's dirty laundry becomes the congregation's agenda; this is the shadow side of befriending congregations. This is the problem from which professional distance protects. What I'm suggesting is that we open up the highway and see ways in which clergy can encourage excellence in community, mutuality in leadership, emotional needs as legitimate subjects, not objects, of concern. My destination is an understanding of how forgiveness works so that its powers may be realized.

Most women know something of this process in congregations. A number of men know how to do it, too, and the congregations they lead flourish. They have gotten past the ideology, the cant, the quaint and predictable shaking of the head when the subject of "the people" comes up and everyone, professionally, agrees that we can't depend on them.

For me power resides in depending on our congregations. If we don't like them, then we won't be able to depend on them. They will be partners with us through the thicket, but will let us go our own way. If we don't like them, we have to understand why. Who might we like if we don't like the people in our congregations? A friend of mine told me that congregations are a wonderful collection of the worst people in each community and the best ones. I think that this is correct. If we dislike the members of our parish, we may not like people period. It is not as though the law firm or library staff or faculty or road crew is any better. We have to assume, in fact, that a congregation has a slight edge over other groups. It gathers under religious principles which, properly understood, have the capacity to judge our pettiness and uphold our goodness. All groups gather around principles, but presumably congregations' principles are more rich and full than those of most groups. Our allegiance to the Gospel, rather than to some other credo, assumes that we will be more capable of internal criticism, of upholding the paradox inherent in other systems and in ourselves. Otherwise, what are we doing sailing under this Gospel banner?

I am frequently accused of being romantic about congregations. People think I don't see how petty and mean and nasty some congregations are to some ministers. I do see this; I see it all the time. Frankly, I see more of it than I can bear. But I see the relationship with congregations as a love affair. The only solution to problems in love is more love. The only way to heal some of these monster congregations is more love. When we remember that we have love above and beyond our own to draw on and instead use our professional skills to erect fences, we don't have to be threatened by the monsters. We become nonchalant towards pettiness. Applying more would mean getting involved, perhaps taking direct action against the monsters on behalf of the congregation. We would use tougher love, not sloppy love, and sometimes the monsters would be healed.

If we are stuck in critiquing our congregations, if we are hurt by what they have done or are doing to us, if we stick to our one lane and fight it out, we are just feeding the monster. We become part of the triangle and accept its terms. We have the capacity to take the fight to higher ground or different ground. The process of forgiveness requires that we draw liberally from this capacity.

Power blends agency and communion. Women are displaying this blend in a delightful pattern of consensus. Mary E. Hunt joins many other women in a reclamation of the idea of agency. In an article in *Waterwheel* entitled "Agents with Integrity," she expands the notion of agency as meaning "one who makes or does something on her/his own terms."[2] She says that women religious agents do three things: "We name experience on our own terms; we make decisions on the basis of these experiences; we form communities of accountability in which our decisions are critiqued and supported." This is excellent advice for clergy. Within our congregations we find the communities of accountability in which our decisions are critiqued and supported. In such communities communion finds a rightful balance with agency.

Hunt expresses the obvious when she says that "many of us have never experienced five minutes of agency in patriarchal religious traditions. As a Roman Catholic woman I cannot think of an instance where my religious agency has been respected within the institutional framework. . . ." Terminology is crucial here. If God is considered outside of our own authority, the development of agency is quickly seen as getting the power to set your own terms. Some of us have found out how to set our own terms; now these terms need to be put into action.

Adam Michnik, the great Polish poet and politician, tells us that if we want to be free, we must act our way to freedom. You want free elections, he told the Polish people, conduct free elections. You want free speech, speak freely. We could apply this wisdom to ourselves. If we want congregations that release the capacities of many, including and especially women, then we will have to build them. We will have to activate the terms we have set.

Of course, we may get fired. That's a given. Never fool yourself into thinking that people want to be liberated. But caring more about the congregation than we do about getting fired gives us a piece of power. We are, after all, professionals.

The road to power is both exquisitely simple and complicated. If clergy as a community were to make it our goal to leave churches stronger than when we arrived, we would begin to see power in both our failures and our successes. We would cease finding community only among ourselves and cast our lot more firmly with our congregations. The word on the street is always that the former minister was a jerk and that we have to spend years cleaning up his/her messes. Come on. Can this possibly be true? Does it disregard the congregation's own set of decisions, its own need to be a certain way? I don't think ministers are that responsible for the way congregations are. Congregations are the way they are because of who they are and how they want to be. We have some power to lead them, to be sure. That power increases every time we act consciously toward our goals, and it decreases every time we get snared in the congregation's confusion about where it is heading. Even failure to achieve our goals can be a form of agency; we can still talk about why we failed. We can evaluate the situation until the cows come home. Out loud, of course. The powerlessness will become power later on. Again, if power is conceived as the ability to realize our capacities within the congregation, we can tolerate some frustration of immediate goals to allow the long-term unfolding to work its way.

Making a congregation conscious of mutually set goals, and forgiving them as often as you forgive yourself for not quite heading there full steam ahead, is professional ministry. That is what we are there to do. We acquaint people with the road. We travel the road with them. We join them in finding God along the road. We don't have to like all the people all the time to travel with them. Some days, weeks, months, years, we don't even have to make progress. We just have to know where we are going. More often than not our "cheek" is turned towards getting the congregation to identify its goals and preparing ourselves to follow them: this is mutuality. We may find ourselves, as some do, asking the same question for years: is this fight what we hope for our congregation? Is it goal number one around here to keep new/young/different folk out of power and older folk in power? If not this year or next year, when might that change? If this dialogue works, we all have the power we need to realize our common capacities. Even Lech Walesa realized that the new cabinet in formation had to include some old leaders. Almost all mutuality is negotiated. If the conversation doesn't work, we have a fight over one lane.

Being *with* others, not *for* others, is the main challenge women are making to status quo ministry. Men in ministry have a different struggle with this matter than we do. Many men already are deep into the contradiction between their gender style and their faith style. Achieving power *with* rather than power *over* is more of an uphill journey for a man than for a woman. We still believe the conventional wisdom that *power over* is how ministry should be done. So many women get accused of being too "with" and incapable of being "over." The paradigm has to change before the justice of a two-way street is established.

The masculine paradigm of agency unmitigated by communion is an obstacle for both men and women in getting power in congregations. It keeps the fight all jammed up in one lane where there is no room to move except against each other. Women, and men, have the resources to open up the fight in such a way so that both congregations and ministers have more power through the transformations of repentance. The first step, as Alice Walker puts it, is to "adore the people."[3] To adore the people well is ministry. To adore them so well that when your team member follows you, he/she can tell that the people have been adored by observing the fruits of their spirits. Adoring is less about liking people at every moment than it is a promise to stay in the process of repentance with them. Not only congregations will be well fed under this arrangement of power-sharing and enhancing, but also ministers themselves.

NOTES

1. Parker Palmer, "Learning is the Thing for You: Renewing the Vitality of Religious Education," *Weavings* (September/October 1989): 24.

2. Mary E. Hunt, "Agents with Integrity," *Waterwheel* (Spring/Summer 1989): 1.

3. Alice Walker, "Goodnight, Willie Lee, I'll See You in the Morning," *Poems* (New York Dial Press, 1979), 40.

CHAPTER 15

Climbing Out of the Fishbowl: Three Pictures of Power

Three pictures may help demonstrate the shape that conscious, mutual capacity-building takes. The first two take place in the parish ministry; the third is a nonlocal picture of ministry. Each illustrates the paradigm shift that power will take as women realize their capacities in ministry.

Picture one: A ministerial candidate was interviewing for a pastor's position. While touring the church, his eye was offended by a large American flag placed between the altar and the crucifix. In his interview, he said, "That flag has to go." The search committee remembers thinking right away that they didn't like this "frank" feature of his personality. But everything else was right about the man, so he was chosen. About three months into his first year, the new pastor preached a sermon about the flag. The sermon was theologically sound and showed a great deal of care in its preparation. It was a three-pronged critique of the flag's central position in the sanctuary. The same three points appeared in the pastor's column in the newsletter the same month. The insiders had endured the sermon with but a few gastrointestinal disturbances at Sunday dinner. But the outsiders, those who had not heard the sermon because they did not attend church, read the article as a throwing down of a gauntlet, which is exactly what it was.

The *brouhaha* that followed marred the honeymoon of this particular rookie. He had many years of experience in the ministry, but he was a professional rookie. Probably he had had too much success in his earlier years and had not learned to respect congregations.

Predictably, the insiders sided with the outsiders against the new minister. He was devastated. Their disloyalty to him and their loyalty to their fellow congregants felt like betrayal. Thus began the new pastor's projection on to the previous pastor. He had been a *pater familias,* an old softie, wouldn't know a theological principle if it hit him in the face. He had pandered to the congregation. Thus, he was the source of the present problem. It was the new pastor's job to wean the congregation from this authoritarian ghost and, by God, he would do it.

The scrambling that went on for the one lane of power that was open in that church lasted seven years. The congregation went from 700 members to 500 members; giving took a similar dive. After about three years, the conference sent in a team to help. After a series of meetings, the flag was moved to the left of the altar about ten feet. Just about everyone was miserable.

What the minister hadn't realized was that the congregation experienced the judgment against the flag as judgment against themselves. Some of those people had real feelings about the flag; others did not, but did have feelings about the status quo. They understood what the minister was saying about God and country, but they felt put down by the way he said it. It was as if he thought they were stupid and that they had to change before he would like them. He seemed to think he was better and smarter than they were.

What the minister experienced was the awful truth that people in congregations prefer each other to him. The loyalties are, thank God, lateral, rather than vertical. Lay people are less capable of conflict than ministers are; they refuse to stand against each other and, in that refusal, often stand against change in the status quo. Even the craziest and most estranged member of most congregations is listened to more than the pastor at his/her most poetic. Protest beats poetry at every turn. The frustration of capacities of the protester fuels the frustration of the capacities of the pastor unless another lane is opened up so that both the pastor and the protester have room to operate. Pastors need to begin to understand this tightly woven fabric of community as a strength, as something you'd want to achieve if it wasn't there.

When we respect as strength the friendships and bonds in congregations, we stop competing with them. We do not experience people sticking together as betrayal. Rather we join with them and become a part of that glue ourselves. We take a normal nonhierarchical position within the community. Our specialness is that we come and go, and before we go we may have a hand in making those bonds even more complex, loving, and inclusive than they were when we came. We help our congregations catch the wind at their back, we blow into their strength, which is community built by their capacity. We don't expect to get out in front and "lead" them. Perhaps this is another way of understanding the concept of servanthood.

Picture two: Another minister went to a church which also had a flag prominently displayed. She too was offended by it and what it meant. Two years into her ministry there, during a scheduled conversation about the decoration of the sanctuary, she asked the worship board a series of questions, one of which had to do with the position of the flag. Half of the board expressed their doubt about the propriety of a flag so centrally located. The other half said they liked it there and liked what it meant. No one could remember how it got there or who put it there. One person said wisely that as a worship board they had the power to move or change it, but he wasn't sure they should use that power without further consultation. He asked the minister to preach a sermon on the flag. The minister asked the chair of the board to prepare something for the next newsletter to alert the congregation to the board's consideration of the issue. In its search-but-not-destroy mission, the article would locate any persons in the congregation with strong feelings about the flag. A woman whose husband died in World War II wrote an impassioned letter about how her experience of worship was enhanced by the flag. The minister referred to it in her sermon.

About six months later, the flag was moved about ten feet to the right of the altar. One person, an outsider, a veteran, a man known for his ability to cause trouble, withdrew his pledge. Members of the Board of Worship shrugged their shoulders: they knew they had done the best they could and were on firm ground. They had respected everyone's feelings; their only regret was that this man did not respect their process.

Such a process is a necessary preparation for public ministry. I would not want to depend on the first congregation for community work. Even if you were able to involve them in a public issue or witness, God only knows what would happen. The fabric of trust was so weak that the congregation would probably embarrass itself publicly. None of them even knew about the first step of admitting wrong much less the second of forgiving each other. The second congregation is clearly in training for mission. They are building capacity by learning how to mutually and consciously become who they want to become. They are developing an identity as a congregation that shares power, has open processes, expects to experience forgiveness, and is able to endure conflict. This congregation has the capacity for mission.

When we talk about power, we are talking about both the process of not frustrating capacities and the process of realizing them.

Much of our time will be spent in staying out of the way of the congregation, of not riling them up over our agendas, of respecting their right to do what they are going to do with their church. The proactive stance is much harder to achieve. For many congregations, it takes years to develop enough internal capacity and trust to operate publicly. Obviously our time with congregations is dedicated to building that capacity—not so that congregations grow and meet budgets and enjoy each other, but precisely so that over time public possibilities open up.

The same congregation that democratically moved their flag a few feet to the side of the altar has just won a serious battle with the city in favor of a public housing project in their neighborhood. Their soup kitchen is training "clients" to serve in it. Their widows' group is bringing in others from the local senior housing project. The lanes are opening up. They are developing the capacity for mission. Their private capacities turn naturally to the public sphere. But this takes time to achieve. Just as some people won't invite their friends to church because they're afraid they will be embarrassed, many churches won't do public ministry for fear that the internal "family" feuds will become public knowledge.

Power is the ability to have some control over our worlds just as authority is the ability to have some control over ourselves. Personal power is a contradiction in terms. Congregations that have the capacities to release each other's gifts become capable over time of public ministry. They become capable of having some power over the world of their community. For most it is local power; for others it embraces the national or international. Somehow, people have learned to get along with each other, not perfectly but well enough to head for a public goal and achieve it. We as pastors don't need power to survive conflicts with our own leaders or to survive our own moral lapses; we need power to realize our purposes in ministry.

In every assignment, we may not experience the joy of fully realized parishes. But we do have the responsibility of moving congregations down these roads and through these processes of repentance so that whoever follows us has something more to work with.

Picture three: In my denomination we have a socialist insurance policy. In other words, we are self-insured and I love it. I take special care of my medical bills precisely because I know that by keeping costs down, I am helping others and eventually myself in the process of staying well. If some of our bills go up, all of our bills go up. If some of us are sick, the rest of us pay for it. There's a self-interest motive behind this wellness model. If our goal is to develop parishes capable of public power, and I think that is our goal in mission terms, we are also self-insured. The wellness model applies to parishes as well as to health. The more power each of us can realize, the greater the health and effectiveness of the whole. Unleashing our capacities, in the end, makes us well.

Out of the Fishbowl

As pastors we have power to the degree that we are capable of worship. In fact, this capacity to worship, to get on our knees and not feel ridiculous, to know forgiveness, seems to me to be a prerequisite for developing a community strong enough to have power in the public world.

Most pastors, of course, don't worship. On Sunday mornings we perform. We practice our trade. If we go to someone else's service, we spend the time in an extended critique of the service: *Why did she choose that hymn? Do they really not have inclusive language here? What an awkward turn of phrase in the pastoral prayer.* Our choosing to stay in the performance mode and to "help" other people worship is evidence that we are not ready for power. Our capacities are not being released as gift but rather acted out. We are ministry machines. We ply our trade. The fact that we use prayers rather than hammers, songs rather than spades doesn't matter. We are still working. Some of this is inevitable. The refinement of our skills in worship is right there for everyone to see. There is more than one fishbowl aspect to ministry. Sometimes, it may be necessary to fake a beatific smile as we sing "Holy, Holy, Holy," especially if we are redoing the sermon. We can't worship in every way at every time. Nor can we expect ourselves to endure some of the liturgies that our colleagues put together. I am only now becoming able to find God through the thicket of the sexist language I hear in my association. I am developing a nonchalance toward it so that after the service when I discuss the matter with the perpetrators, my behavior tends towards the nonviolence of hoped-for change rather than the violence of demanded change. The course in forgiveness is a long one, and its goals are not always reached.

But over time, and at least in our own congregations, we should be able to worship. If we can't worship in our own services on Sunday mornings, then we should attend another service at another time of the week. In Philadelphia there was a great gospel service every Sunday night right on the corner where I lived. I worked in the morning and at night I worshipped. The capacity to release our

gifts is very much the capacity to be well channeled by God. Good
worship is openness to the Spirit. Disciplining this openness is crucial to capacity. Otherwise the idolatries flow and grow. It is we
whose skills are so fine who are doing the ministry and not God. It
is we and our talent that are making this church work so well and
not God. When we can't or don't find the time for praise, for the
act of forgiveness and resolution, for deep hearing of the Word, for
the offering of our gifts, our whole ministries get skewed. Letting
go of ourselves and our performance in worship gives us the
power we need to make it through the week. We absolutely are like
all lay people in this way. Our need for God may not be more than
theirs, but it is certainly not any less. Scratch a powerful minister
and you will find one who has learned how to worship. The power
they are using is God's.

Learning to worship will help us with the notorious fishbowl
problem. Ministers, both male and female, are all placed in fishbowls by their congregations. Congregations use us to be their am-
bassadors with God. They use us to do their clean work. We are
supposed to believe that the Gospel applies to ordinary economic
life; they are not. They know better because they're part of the *real*
world. So we are suspended in the spiritual, set aside to say and believe the things they have no intention of saying or believing.
Clergy are supposed to be better than other people. We all know
this set up. Their extramarital affair was something that couldn't be
helped given the pressures of their life; ours is a violation of the
commandments. Never mind that the commandment for clergy is
the same as that for laity. When we position ourselves above worship, and above the need for God, we play right into this mentality.
We climb right into the fishbowl.

Adam Michnik, the Polish poet, advocates playing cards as revolution when you can't snap governments open. Here he would also
see the power we already have and recommend that we use it. He
would advocate climbing out of the fishbowl. It is the same thing as
opening up another lane, setting other terms for the discussion. No
longer are our capacities frustrated, but they are released. That is
power. Does the use of this kind of power mean that we will
change the world? No. God's agencies will do that. We may or may
not be a piece of them. However, if we do not use these kinds of
powers—those that come from worship and from caring for our
people in as skillful a way as possible—we can be assured that the
world will certainly *not* change. And just as bad, we will live our
life in a traffic jam, willing victims of its noise and hatred. Or to put
it another way, we will spend our life underwater, being observed,

being judged, being used. The choices are clear and set before us in the first testament's language as matters of life and death. In the second testament, they are flesh and spirit. In the living testament of our lives they show up as open lanes, empty fishbowls, and re-pentant power.

CHAPTER 16

Getting to Where You Said You Were Going

A major problem for clergy who care about power is accountability. Sometimes it appears that we live in a self-referential tunnel where we make and meet our own goals. Such independence is counter-productive to the development of communities. In order for us as clergy to get the power we need to avoid the frustration of our capacities and fulfill the vows we made at ordination, we need the help of a simple job description.

If you set out from Riverhead for Montauk and arrive an hour or so later, you know you have reached your goal. Neither a parish pastor nor a parish enjoys the luxury of such certainty. Things may "feel good" for the insider, but outsiders may not be a part of the good feelings. The goal of community is elusive. The budget may be reached, but contain insufficient resources for the needy or for the proper maintenance of church property. The goal of financial stability is tricky. The Bible may be read every Sunday in worship, but the people may be biblically illiterate. Attendance may be strong at the youth group, but the program content weak. In the midst of all this confusion, the pastor and congregation may not even know which of contradictory, but desirable, goals to aim for. People may not have decided to get to Montauk in the first place.

Parishes and pastors reach some of their goals, but rarely all. Our desires are always more rich and complex, more shifting and special than simply arriving at Montauk. We don't always arrive; sometimes we arrive late. Sometimes we arrive, but we are unaware that we are "there." We may think we are on the road to repentance, but actually have driven into a ditch. This often is true when it comes to discerning the presence of the Holy Spirit. Many people think the Spirit is only present when the waters are smooth; the biblical account argues differently, announcing the presence of the

Spirit in troubled and smooth waters, ruffled and smooth feathers, in journey as well as destination.

Parish reality is sufficiently complicated to permit getting stuck with vague goals. The chaos factor, the human factor, the Holy Spirit factor sanctions most clergy in their vagueness. But while affirming flexibility, we also may need to question it from time to time. Vagueness may be a hiding place, a protection from the responsibilities of power, a cloaking in the fashionable garb of flexibility. Power for a parish exists when the Gospel is spoken and heard, when biblical realities become institutional realities. This meaning of incarnation, the institutionalization of the absolute priority of loving God and each other, is an awesome accountability. To privatize this love by keeping its references only to the self, rather than seeking the power to make it public, is to violate the Gospel in a fundamental way. When only the pastor is clear about where she/he is going, accountability is impossible.

At the least, power is the capacity to get to where you said you were going. It is to arrive at Montauk if you said you were going there. It is to institutionalize love if that's how you read the Gospel. Parish goals need to be as concrete as going to Montauk if the responsibilities of power are to be taken seriously. We get to institutionalize love here, not there—now, not later.

Yes, there are obstacles along the way. The concretizing of goals in a parish is not just inhibited by its implicated realities. It is also inhibited by fundamental confusions in the minister's orientation to power. There is still a feeling of naughtiness in talking about power, although increasingly pastors are preaching about it, and neither clergy nor parishes faint at its possibilities anymore. More likely these days, so deeply in decline is old-line religion, people prefer power and are thrashing about trying to get it. Between our decline and the ascendancy of cultural aggressions, Protestantism, at least, has pretty well decided that God legitimates power with a few precautions. If we don't get hung up on it, idolize it, or make it a priority, but rather put power to use toward stated ends, we're ready.

Thus relieved of our previous idolatries of weakness, we are prepared to engage the more serious difficulties. For clergy that weakness shows up in vagueness. We are on a fence between professional accountabilities and particular accountabilities. We are self-actualizing and validate ourselves by how well we perform our tasks, regardless of consequences, or we are accountable in covenant and judge ourselves by consequences, regardless of how well we perform our tasks. We declare that we will reach certain measurable goals, say ten new members per year, or we declare that we are much too professional to ever commit to such a worldly goal.

Obviously this professional/practical scale is a spectrum. Most of us are a bit sore between the legs so long have we straddled the fence. If our vagueness about goals originates in this legitimate confusion, perhaps our soreness is not all bad. It may be preferable to the soreness of stating goals that require achievement when achievement seems so impossible.

The role of clergy is both professional and particular. We preach in the context of the one holy catholic church, stating the Gospel as well as we can, week in and week out, and our words are judged by their faithfulness to the text. We are frequently deeply in touch with our commitment to the church over time and to our obligations to those clergy who will follow us. Maybe if we speak these gospels now, someone will listen. Ten years from now our successor will be grateful to us. The fact that some of the other people listening today will call for one of those famous congregational meetings where "many" people will report disturbance should not affect us as professionals. But because we are not only professionals, but also particular pastors to particular people to whom we are accountable, what happens at that real or threatened meeting is vital to our covenant in the moment. So we ride the fence some more.

The ability to get concrete while being held in the arms of principle is a fine example of that famous both/and to which we are called. I am bothered by women friends who get so bogged down in details that they can't even remember what the purpose of the church fair was in the first place, so buried are they in strawberry potholders. These same women are still reeling from one negative comment by one person three weeks ago, so untutored are they in the true numerology of critical comments in the ministry. (The true numerology is 1000 critical comments per year, half disguised as kindness, another third being just plain stupid, and the final fraction requiring that we take them utterly seriously because the person has a point, so well do they know the Achilles heel in us and so godsent are they in calling our attention to how much it has been showing lately.) Likewise, there are many men who irritate precisely because they have transcended the particular so thoroughly that they can't be torn away from their computer screen, so busy are they listing and analyzing the goals of the church fair and noting accountabilities reached. These guys wouldn't be caught dead near a potholder made in the shape of a strawberry. They haven't listened to an off-the-wall comment from anyone in their parish for years.

Deciding where we are going is the prelude to power. Parish pastors are going to the fence of ministry, there both to judge our own fidelities to the text and to make some things happen in the parish. We are above consequences in our performance in certain ways. We may be doing a good job while the church membership is decreasing. We may also be the cause of that decline. We are also bound by consequences. Sometimes that very hunger, that whoring after approval to which much ministry actually goes, causes plenty of seemingly attractive consequences. (I have yet to meet a denominational executive who was not attracted to the growth of a parish, even if that parish was being unfaithful to the text.) Many churches are growing precisely because the Gospel has been disguised as guilt-free do-goodism. Holy water is poured on capitalism and culture using buckets filled with the pastor's need to be liked. This growth is lauded everywhere, but it hardly represents the power of the Gospel. Only a piece of the Gospel is served when people feel so comforted. Serving that piece may be better than lots of other things in this cold world, but its inadequacy must be realized by those wanting to unleash power for the Gospel in their parish and world.

Power for the pastor comes in the assurance that the Gospel is being spoken and being heard. The place for which we are heading, and for which we need power to reach, is fidelity to the Gospel and its actualization among us and our people in the here and now. Here we land on a fence again: sometimes we speak the Gospel in word and deed and realize that no one is listening, and that those who are are offended. Other times we frame the Gospel so that it can be heard. Other times we build a community of openness to its truth slowly over time. In these times when the Gospel must compete with an aggressive and greedy culture, I am afraid our power in ministry is to prepare the community to hear, to heighten the contrast and deepen the contradictions. It may always have been so. That also may be a cop out, as though preparation would work to open hearts to the Word of God. It may be that conflict is what does the opening, and so we may as well speak what we think is true and take our lumps. As a fence straddler, I believe we should be doing both all the time. I have learned to enjoy ridiculous postures. Sometimes we actually need the courage to be wishy-washy, the capacity to be so engaged in the immediate situation that we abandon principles willingly on behalf of persons. At other times we will need the courage to be firm, to abandon persons on behalf of principles. On occasion, flags will move six inches from the center of the sanctuary after the long and delightful process that makes room for both persons and principles.

Taking our lumps and preparing communities means that we will be both liked and disliked. This tension is necessary for the possibility of power. The community may have to get power over us and through us and with us. Our part in this tension is to hold up our end. Thus clarity about our ends is crucial.

I love job descriptions. For women in ministry they are especially important. Our gender places us firmly on the side of unconditional, immeasurable love; mothers are the only ones who make sense next to their sons on death row. If we approach our ministries without conditions and without measurements, however, we soon go berserk. To describe a job is to acknowledge some limits on our care; whether or not the job ever actually fits its description is another matter. Likewise, we gain access to power by focusing our energies. There is no point in having power over everything. That is totalitarian. To have power in the places where we and others have covenanted to have it, to get to the places where we have said we want to go, is a decision against totalitarianism and for standing our ground in our time and place in community. Job descriptions give limits, and limits are our friends in ministry.

Over the years, I have operated somewhat within the confines of the following job description. In each situation, the congregation and community have modified it. The modifications have been the real energy of the place, the things that people really wanted to see happen. Nevertheless, it has been my responsibility to have a guide even when the people didn't see a need for it.

From my experience, the parish job seems to divide into four parts. One is pastoral care; the second is worship; the third is what I have now named *Tikkun,* the Hebrew word for repairing and restoring of that which is broken, the care of the fabric of the place, what many others call administration or stewardship of the heritage; and the fourth is the work of justice, the release of the community's care for the poor. I used to think of the first three as private and the last as the public aspect of ministry, but I no longer see it that way. The work of pastoral care is on behalf of the congregation's ministry in the world. Worship involves the public Words of God. Frequently the work of justice is caring for persons, especially caring for the people who work for justice in significant ways. They may be the most spiritually starved people around, so few are their caretakers and so fundamental their tasks.

In pastoral care, I usually divide the congregation's family "units" by the forty-eight working weeks of the year; that gives me the number of calls I must make per week. In a parish of about 300 members, that means that if I do three calls a week, I'll see the entire congregation each year. I think this "wellness" calling is probably the most important thing a pastor can do. Through calling we get to know each other; the basic relationships are nurtured and developed. Clergy who don't do this kind of calling probably don't know what's going on with their people and therefore probably can't discern the direction the community is going. Not knowing how the breezes are blowing for people in their own lives at their own developmental stage is terrifying to a pastor. A vacuum is created, and ministry in a vacuum has been known to destroy a pastor. He or she will have no relationships on which to feed.

At the same time that the wellness calling is going on, crisis care must continue. We should always die with our people. When they get close to death, we should join the family vigil and give it all we have. This accompanying of people across the Jordan is part of speaking the Gospel. Doing this, of course, interferes with accomplishing our daily tasks. But death clearly is one of those occasions when our schedules need interruption. We should always be prepared for interruptions. We don't have to like them, but we should be ready for them. Similarly, the care of the sick is crucial to pastoral care. As a rule of thumb, a life-threatening illness deserves one hospital visit per day, a chronic illness a contact every other day by phone or, better, in person, and medical tests and their results ongoing careful monitoring. We want people to know that we care. If we can't manage all of this, it is our duty to get others in the parish to help us. They also have signed up to care pastorally for each other, and it is our job to activate and inform them. Particularly when the hospitals are far away, this kind of care can be formidable. Then the telephone will have to do.

A final element of pastoral work is the care and feeding of our lay leadership. At least monthly we should take a good, long look at the people who are the elected and informal leaders of the congregation. How are they holding up? Do they feel appreciated? So often the people who are giving the most in a parish receive the least pastoral care; this is a costly mistake.

Under the category of worship, there is preaching and the various sacraments of wedding, funeral, baptism, and the like. If these are done well, much else will fall in place. It is at these points, rather than the much-vaunted leadership development retreat, that people are strengthened for their work in the parish and the world. Pastors do well turning away from the busywork of programs toward sacramental ministries. If we keep the sacraments strong, there will be people who will keep the Sunday School strong. Very often I find ministers, particularly women, with their love of detail, meddling in program affairs. If the congregation can't find the lay leadership it needs to mount a good Christian education program or women's program or music program, then those programs should not happen. It really is as simple, and disturbing, as that.

Tikkun is a fancy Hebrew word to describe all that which is not fancy. Letting the glazier in to fix the window. Locating the red bowl that the women's fellowship needs. Assuring that the former officers are properly thanked. Assuring that everyone concerned with an issue is informed of a change in its status. Nurturing secretaries and other paid employees. Remembering to get reimbursed for money handed out at the door.

We will have a tendency to think we are too good to do these things. We are not. Done well, they are the glue of community. Done poorly, they create separations and alienation and a kind of privilege of the spiritual over the material that is alien to the Gospel's urge to incarnate. They need to be in the job description.

Finally, the work of justice, the intentional development of public community so that it incarnates the love of Christ for the world, is a crucial part of a job description for a minister and a congregation. It is often the part that gets squeezed out because members are so vocal and nonmembers are not. The church, however, is not a club. Its doors are open, its boundaries permeable to the public. Part of the mission budget of a congregation really should include the pastor's time. Becoming intentional about making some difference to the poor is necessary in every community. One way to do it is to follow the local minority leaders around and to see the world with their eyes. Another is to choose an issue and become the town's watchdog on it; churches are great at initiating public activity. A third is to develop over time a strong social action committee within the parish. Surely keeping strong connections with regional and national ecumenical organizations is vital to our care for justice. These organizations depend so much on local parishes for funds and for nourishment. Keeping them alive is very much the mission of the local church.

Ministers will call these four pieces of their job by different names. They may or may not divide into four parts. I have found good balance in my ministry when I sit down on Monday and organize myself so that I'm doing all four aspects. I want to do a little bit of each every day, but I won't do it unless I spend a few minutes each day dedicating myself and my calendar to them. If a minister were to spend ten hours a week on each category, both balance and power would be achieved. More time is rarely needed. If we find that more time is needed, we probably have tipped the scale in one direction and we need to confer with others about whether that is an appropriate tip. I have a tendency to overdo in the justice area and thus the 25 percent rule helps me know when to say no. If I want to do more than a normal week's work, and as I have said before I really don't want to at all, then I can tip the scale in favor of my interests. To be conscious about these decisions on a daily and weekly basis, and to have partners who are willing and able to tell us what they think is going on, permits a minimal level of accountability. That accountability is a prelude to power.

Each part of my job description has as its immediate goal the building of a strong congregation in a strong community. Building communities requires a confidence that if I get sick or in trouble, someone will stand by. Building communities requires that the Word is understood and spoken with as much creativity and freshness as we can muster. Building communities depends on taking care of business and developing a confidence over time that business will be taken care of. Building communities is a constant dispersal of power, both in the ways we manage our internal affairs and in the level of participation of the wider community in the public decisions that affect its life. One way to read the Word of God is that the work of God is to create human community, and that it does so by caring and by dispersing the power to care. Someone once said that God's activity in history was the constant, continuous dispersal of power.

The work of the pastor is not all activity. It is also guarding the margins of time so that our powers of discernment and judgment stay strong, alert, well stimulated. It is important not to be initiating all the time, but to receive the initiations of others. That may sound trite, but it is not. Overcrowding is death to community building; we lose time to enjoy each other.

Just because a job description is in place, and is being implemented rather than occupying the space under J in the file, doesn't mean that the ministry is simplified. All it means is that the accountability side of the fence has been strengthened in partnership with the other side where our ordination vows live. It is an excellent partnership, one that has every chance of reaching its stated destination. Power in community is found on the road to our Montauks. Rather than watching capacities frustrated and vows belittled, job descriptions help people get to where they said they wanted to go.

PART IV

Authority

CHAPTER 17

Authority as a Two-Way Street: An Introduction

The problem I face with authority in my ministry parallels the problem I face in raising my sons and daughter. Everything I read on raising healthy children in a nonsexist way tells me to make sure my daughter has the advantages of being a boy. No one is urging me to raise my boys so that they have the advantages of being a girl. Are there advantages to being a girl? I think so. But no one wants to elevate them in the way that male advantages are elevated. These advantages have very little authority. They are invisible to the untrained eye. So is the authority of women in ministry: when we try to restring our pearls, we discover that half of them are hidden and the other half are missing.

To me authority is the ability to control yourself, particularly to be a partner in establishing the criteria by which you, and others, will judge who you are. Child development experts describe the process as the gradual internalization of values. I must train my eye to find the authority of women. We don't create authority; it is not something we make up ourselves. Rather it is the public process of value determination, of cultural formation, of wrestling the angels and the demons for the criteria that are important. The masculine and feminine are interlocking sets of criteria. The feminine criteria are buried; they don't carry as much weight as the masculine. I want to exhume them, to bring them closer to the surface of our culture so that we all, both men and women, may travel a two-way street, going a feminine or a masculine direction as the moment calls for.

The authority of women has at least five faces. Our language can be authoritative; what we don't say, our secrets, can also be authoritative. I see authority in our ability to care and in our ability to offer hospitality. I see how both curse and blessing are on our table, and how humor negotiates the distance between them.

As I look at these five faces, I will try very hard not to pit feminine authority against men. I'm looking for a two-way street to open some paths that men can travel in the same way that women already travel so many masculine paths. There is no reason why well-developed critical capacity and well-developed caring capacity cannot coexist. There is nothing that says that the masculine authority of strength can't partner with weakness. If anything, the various so-called opposites of different authorities are strengthened by meeting their partner.

I want men and women to share their toys, for each to become comfortable with both the quiet poke of a push mower and the sound of a serious engine. I see boys playing with dolls as much as girls play with trucks. I see male and female children walking down the road dressed and dazzling with baseball bats in hand. Such a world I could join Alice Walker in adoring. Rather than merely seeking justice and equality, as important as they are, I'd like to find all the possibilities inherent in an androgynous world. For that to me is true justice, that fullness that comes when we are able to adore the whole spectrum of gender.

Women in ministry have been doing ministry with trucks and baseball bats. Like my daughter we play a lot of cowboy and trains and doctor. (In seminary, I just loved it when I was taught not to "identify" with the "client"! It was like dying and landing on Mars. I had no idea how not to identify. And still don't.) Is it safe for us to do ministry differently? No, I think not, not if safety means keeping our jobs. To get to that level of safety, criteria must be found that will expand ministry to fill more than one lane. Men should be more comfortable playing with dolls. We will know we have achieved a fully empowered gender spectrum when we see boys being encouraged to be like girls with the same vigor girls are now encouraged to cross over into the boy's lane. Mutually reinforcing authorities will be achieved when we do ministry with as much emphasis on communion as now is placed on agency.

Frederick Douglas describes a process for getting to authority: "The limits of oppression are determined by the oppressed themselves." Imagine that. We begin to develop authority by determining the limits to our own oppression. We start by having our own conversation with the criteria.

But part of what keeps us from engaging in the process Douglas describes is this: we are co-dependent with sexism. This new psychological fad exposes an old truth. It shows again that trouble is a two-way street, that reality is constantly negotiable, that women clergy, by not naming and fitting into their own criteria, are a part their our own lack of authority. The folk wisdom that it takes two to tangle can't be well enough understood. When we women become more comfortable with who *we* are, and become more visibly and freely feminine in our approach to ministry, we will open new lanes. They won't be lanes just for us, but lanes for ministry as well. Traffic will flow in many directions.

CHAPTER 18

Who Do We Think God Is?
The Authority of Language

I was trying to explain to my two sons that God is not a boy. Nor is God a girl, said I. I've had plenty of practice talking with people about God and gender. But these two boys were my most difficult audience. One burst into song, imitating a Native American song he had learned in school. The original version with drumbeat is, "The Earth is our Mother; we must take care of her." Jacob's version was new and improved: "The earth is our Father; we must take care of him." For a couple of months, which is long in child time, both boys beat imaginary drums and sang Jacob's version. In this child's play at least one of my life ambitions has been met. My sons, without a violation of their own maleness, understand God's inclusive nature.

The boys refused to be excluded in the divine. They had the chutzpah to keep themselves in, rather than out, theologically. We are like God, they were singing. We are like the earth. The difference here between God and earth is theologically significant, but otherwise not. What my boys heard was the authority. They heard the parental authority and the authority of origins. They wanted a piece of the rock.

Too many women are a bit like my children when it comes to God language. Every time we hear about God the Father we feel excluded. It is not that God is not a father as one of many faces, but rather that God is not only Father. We want a way in on the authority. More and more we are getting inclusive language, the ability to use words in such a way that we are in rather than out. This is a large part of the authority we are developing for ministry.

There will be no such thing as a two-way street until God is understood as part of the spectrum of gender. There will continue to be times when, for the sake of the communion, women will sit through masculine imagery. We don't have to fight every *he, him, his, father, brother, man,* that we hear. Such nitpicking belittles us. But we do have to fight firmly the idea that God is male. Language is frequently good turf for the fight. I think it is more important to have this battle at the level of Sunday School than at the level of the ecumenical meeting, although both sites strike me as good stages. We may not have the energy for multiple battle sites.

In this battle, we first must examine who *we* think God is and whether God is excluding the feminine or not. Once our own relationship with God comprehends the gender spectrum, we secure the authority to "correct" others when they limit God. Sometimes in the very stridency of these language fights, I hear us trying to convince ourselves. It is almost as though we are asking for permission from the world to understand God as male and female, mother and father. No one can stop us from worshipping the God whom we dimly comprehend, who has been revealed to us thus far. Not even exclusive language can do that.

The battles over language are ways of normalizing our experience of being a part of God. Whenever "hes" and "hims" are used, we are abnormalized. We are excluded from godliness. Over time these exclusions take an enormous toll on our ability to define our own criteria. If we are all human beings, but men are like gods and women are not, then we are reduced to a subhuman criteria. Men should make, but we should manage. Men should create and we should clean up. We eventually exclude ourselves, by our little hiding trick, from covenantal responsibilities. We do not co-create with God. We do not join in the processes of salvation. We are not really redeemed. We are not even really forgiven because how can you be forgiven for failing to be a partner with God when you weren't supposed to be one in the first place? We eavesdrop on the holy processes. If we want to come out of the stands, off the stairs where we watch what fun the real human beings are having, we have to insist on language change. Inclusive language is not an accessory to our authority; frequently it is a prerequisite to our authority. Being able to use words to express the way we understand God is like taking algebra before trigonometry. How can we define the criteria by which we are judged if our very language is subhumanizing us and consistently telling us that we are not the type of species that makes such important decisions about itself? Borrowing words to understand God is oppressive; when we consent to such oppression, we violate our humanity and hide in subhumanity.

Because this issue is so "theoretical," so seemingly above the fray, I am including as an appendix a case study of one congregation's process in changing to inclusive language (see Appendix B). I hope it shows the mutuality involved in changing our language and how such change can be healthy for all. If the reader remains un-convinced, I can only offer one more story. A 93-year-old Mennonite woman in Ohio, where the churches separated men and women on either side of the church, decided one Sunday that her whole family, boys and girls, men and women, would sit down together. When asked why she took the first step that changed the entire church's practice from then on, she said, "I and my family will sit together." If we don't have the luxury of the kind of process described in the case study, if we find we must use our language without warning or preparing people, then perhaps we can explain our choice as she explained hers: "I and my family will speak together." Sometimes what it takes to sit together is to sit together. Sometimes what it takes to speak is to speak.

CHAPTER 19

Finding Our Voice:
The Authority of Secrets

Slaves had words in their songs that the master didn't understand. Some slave quilts show maps for the underground railroad. Women don't go this far in deceiving men, but there are similarities. We have codes, we have glances, we have airs. Most men know how hard it is to understand women. Women are like slaves; we are bilingual. Black women are multilingual. We have all learned how to talk "male" and how to talk "female," and some of us know how to talk white and talk black.

When among men, we talk the way they do. We refer to our own objectivity as much as possible. We make generalizations. There are rules to this discourse. If you have a feeling, sneak it in. Talk strong, fast, accurately. Among women subjectivity is the rule. Talk in particulars. Let the feelings run wild. Talk vulnerability, slowly, with lots of question marks at the end of each statement.

Is one way right or wrong? I doubt it. They simply express the spectrum of genuine gender difference. They show how much more positively men, in general, feel about themselves than women, in general, do. Don't you just hate it when women make these gross generalizations? Most women hate men for making generalizations more than for anything else. The substitution of one's self and point of view for the whole probably wins the prize for the most galling of the masculine character traits. And yet, men make a contribution by this deceit; they assume a community as opposed to an isolation. Women assume community at the level of feeling, but often not at the level of language. We are well-guarded slaves.

Women gall by our frequent drowning in the particular. I know he won't leave his wife for me but... I know he beats me all the time and men who beat women keep on beating them unless those women leave them... I'll be at the shower unless it rains... There is a female exceptionalism which results from this captivity to the

particular: we either are or are about to be different from the
crowd. When we are not different from the crowd, we blame ourselves. Our inability to generalize depoliticizes us; it keeps us cap-
tive in the private victim place.

My friend has a difficult husband, a difficult father, and a difficult
bishop, and she thinks it is her problem that she can't get along
with men. Do you see the particular spinning its ugly web? Particulars are the enemy of public ministry. She thinks it must be her
fault that all these things have happened to her. Now that she has
started thinking that way, pretty soon it will be her fault. She will
begin to set up situations to repeat the trouble. Her mistrust of men
will become all encompassing because she can't figure out how to
analyze her problem. Her subjectivity is massively in her way.

For us to obtain authority as women, we must learn the shadow
side of our "feminine" language. We must begin to see how easy it
is to drown in the particular, and we must risk making generalizations. While deeply proud of our subjectivity and its willingness to
see *person* rather than *people,* we also must be aware of how easy it
is to violate community by assuming that every situation is uniquely
individual. It is one of the great ironies that we, who value communion over agency in our very bones, violate community by wallow-
ing so in the subjective particular.

Beginning to name these strictly female problems will go a long
way toward developing a two-way street. There is something we
need from men; the critical capacity to stand apart and generalize
can be very useful. The marvels of the feminine have limits. We
don't need to elevate ourselves or our lanes to perfection. Vulnerability expressed is divine behavior if Jesus is any indicator; vulnerability expressed also turns to strength. We need to own the strength
we have received by being willing to admit that we are not always
so.

The simple act of ending sentences with periods rather than
question marks would take us a long way. If my friend were to say,
"Sexism is really a larger and more serious problem than I have
previously been willing to admit" *period,* rather than, "What is it, do
you think, that I am doing and have done to cause all these men to
dislike me so" *question mark,* imagine the difference. She would
have to face the larger public pain of structures that are evil. Clearly
she prefers the private pain (and control, no matter how illusory)
and the personal responsibility to a recognition of structures that
mean her harm. Known pain is preferable to unknown pain.

If we as women want authority, and mostly we do despite our
own tendencies to shoot ourselves in the foot, then we must acquaint ourselves with the shadow sides of our strengths. We will

have to find a voice for the generalities of our own experience. It won't be enough to find cloisters of female friends in which to "be" ourselves. We must seek positive control over ourselves outside of cloisters; we must seek involvement and participation in the public world. Our goal is full partnership in creation. We already have learned how to talk male talk when it is necessary. We know how to enjoy female talk. Understanding the shadow side of our own talk is crucial to our developing authority. It also may be important to abandon male talk altogether. Of course, we should keep the skill available for camouflage. The world has no intention of changing overnight. But authoritative women would insist on talking their own talk all the time, even among men. At least it is worth an experiment: we should compare the pain and alienation of talking male talk in public and female talk in private with the pain and alienation we suffer just by being ourselves in public.

The penalties in being ourselves in public are fairly easy to list. "She" will be called too emotional, unstable, crazy, subjective. Making generalizations, either positive or negative, about these matters will not be pleasing to the public world. She will not be trusted with positions of so-called authority because she won't feel trustworthy enough to most men. She will not be considered tough enough or firm enough or "distant" enough to handle professional rigors. How can you trust someone who is so well acquainted with her own weakness?

Yet I argue that the list of negative adjectives accurately describes the essence of ministry. Ministry is where love and fear fight it out. Each is an emotion. Ministry is God's interaction with the world. It is unstable and permanently conflicted; it is open-ended, undecided, with all bets still on. As far as the slur of crazy is concerned, it takes only a quick glance to see how desperate an accusation it really is. Who, among us, holds the stone of sanity that they dare throw? *Subjective* is one of those words that David uses to toss at the Goliath of imperial objectivity. Imperialisms of all kinds are the enemies of ministers and ministry, particularly those ministries that happen in the open square of the public world.

Men really are not as tough as they think they ought to be. Very few hold up well to the professional rigors, and if they do, the reason is not their gender, but their capacity to be tender towards their own lack of toughness. Again, the feminine wins a fairly simple victory.

Of course you can win these arguments rationally, but lose everything that matters in the process. The reason is simple. We are now toying with male subjectivity, a vast opaque wilderness of chaotic fear. Men have not taken enough time to understand their own emotions and their own subjectivities and therefore really don't want to hear and see women behaving publicly as though we understood ours. Because men still have the power in ministry, they will punish us professionally if we talk our own language.

But is that punishment worse than what we are already experiencing? Linguistic schizophrenia, hiding our real selves, denying our God-given capacities as though we were ashamed of them? Imitating the mistakes of men in being tough and firm and objective? Our authority has a decision to make here about which path we will choose out of the painful slavery of words.

One time about a dozen women from a neighboring parish came to me and asked for my absolute confidentiality. Stupidly, so eager was I to hear the scoop, I agreed. They reported that their minister was sexually harassing them. In great detail, each described how sexual favors, to him, were traded for penance and forgiveness. They wanted someone to talk to, but they did not want to do anything about the problem, or so it developed after about a half a year of conversations. Each woman was afraid to blow the whistle on this guy. The silence was preferable to speech despite the fact that collectively, publicly, they had everything to gain and almost nothing to lose. Finally, only one woman was left who was willing to blow the whistle. She was coming up in his system as a candidate for the ministry; as she saw it, she was going to get in trouble either way. Either telling or not telling threatened her career. She and I went to his superior who literally put his finger to his lips as soon as we began to talk. The message: silence is so preferable to speech. The congregation as an institution would be so damaged, said he. Finally, a sabbatical and some counseling was arranged for the man in question and the seminarian was protected.

Ever since this experience I am unwilling to give confidentiality until I know what is going on. It has been absolutely fascinating to watch the results. I tell people that I am sure the solution to most private problems is to make them public, to at least speak to another person about them if not to organize for changes in the structure that is beating them down. Generalization has tremendous value, no matter how uncomfortable it makes me or most women. The structure may be marriage. It may be public schools. It may be the mandatory upward mobility of our society that oppresses us. It may be class, race, gender, or all three in excruciating combination. Speech against structures creates change; silence does not. Speech heals; silence does not. Because this is my confidence, the basis of my confidentiality, I refuse the latter in respect for the former.

The institution served by that man was already severely damaged. Fear was beating love. Sure the church could pay its dues and perform the external duties. It was a strong and public congregation, one that I might have been proud to serve. But it severely damaged a dozen, if not more, women in their search for God. It put them off the track. To allow congregations to forego their spiritual tasks in favor of their material tasks is an outrage.

The man responsible for the outrage could not come to terms with his own gender or his own sexuality. He wanted more power than it was right for him to have. His own vulnerability and powerlessness took him across a border; he invaded holy places, and he did so as a holy man. Were the women in his territory more able to find and use their own voices, healing would have been possible for him and for them. The chance for healing was blown by their silence.

When I think of our authority as women, I think of the authority of our secrets, spoken and unsilenced. Some of the secrets are about men, whom we unwisely protect, and some are about ourselves, that we, like men, are also not all we are cracked up to be. We are good at community, but not that good. Like men, we are good at being strong and bold, but not that good. Like slaves, we sing too many songs that the master cannot understand. If we are to be free, we will have to discover a public and an open language.

CHAPTER 20

Keeping Our Promises:
The Authority of Care

The authority that women have is our ability to care. We are good at it. It begins in us as mothers but extends through Meals on Wheels and Greenham Common. Both public and private spheres benefit from our care. We care longer and better than men. Consider the simple fact of our more frequent presence at the bedsides of the dying. Years of hospital visitation have shown me who to expect to see. No matter if the patient is a mother or a mother-in-law, her daughter is the one on duty. Sons visit, daughters stay. (I have just experienced a remarkable exception to this rule that warmed my heart. This man is pioneering the two-way street.)

I overheard a group of older women on the bus in New York complaining about the declining quality of daughters-in-law. They didn't bother to complain about the earlier decline in the quality of sons.

This peculiar female caring capacity is one of the reasons that I am going to shoot the next person who tells me to take care of myself. I know I can't continue to do dishes and talk on the phone forever. An evening will come when I won't have the energy to do my correspondence while watching television. I don't plan to go on like this, not wasting a moment or wanting to. But until my three children are raised and the promises I made to the world are approached and fully engaged (because I don't plan to fulfill them), I don't plan to take care of myself. I plan to take care of my children and my promises.

Too many people accuse me, and many I know, of doing too much. My mother can't stop, and my friends read too many magazines on the fine art of self-care. "Oh, my," they all say about my three children, my full-time job, and my frequent fun, "I just don't know how you do it."

Well, that's the whole point. I don't do it. My vocation is caring,

and every day I fail to realize it. Caring is not something you succeed at; it is simply something you do. I don't finish everything I
start. For every call I make, I can think of two more I should have
made. I leave the phone answering machine on for extensive periods when I am at home. I cut corners. I keep sewing projects in
plastic bags for years just so I can remember that I would enjoy an
evening with busy hands and an empty mind. I triage my entire
desk every few months and literally throw out piles of unanswered
mail. Every few weeks I do the same thing to the telephone list. If
the list of people who need calls returned goes over thirty by Friday, I get nervous. I declare an emergency. And then I pick the five
or so who really need a reply and lose the rest of the pink slips.
Then I forgive myself for not "doing it."

Am I proud of my ability to continue making commitments after
I overextend? You bet. I don't think being overextended is the
sin that the self-care movements purport it to be. Rather I am in-
clined to locate the sin in self-care, in always being so careful not to
get tired, in perpetually focusing on the limits rather than the possibilities in your own energy. Do I get tired? Yes and frequently.
Worse—and this really makes my New Age friends cluck—I even
get sick. Colds, flus, minor aches and pains, once a serious illness.
When I learned that I was not going to die tomorrow, which fear I
indulged quite thoroughly, I went back to my old bad habits of filling up the appointment book and trying to have as much fun as
possible at the same time. I find the time to be quiet and prayerful
daily, I find the time to write almost as often, I am led to my garden
for several good sessions with the earth a week, and I have an active social life. The ability to care does not mean that you don't
have fun or that you don't care for yourself. People seem to fear
caring for others because of its threat to caring for self, but the
threat is mental, not actual. Jesus put it as losing your life so you
could gain it, and this process seems more true to me than the
veiled threats of the self-care movements. Moreover, I think most
women join me in these habits and even these beliefs. My experience is that women have the strength to care; we just need other
people to care with us rather than getting in the way of our caring.

I make no claim to being the world's greatest mother, but at a
minimum, my children don't have my unhappiness to contend with
when they get home in the afternoon. I love them deeply and enjoy
every minute I can get with them unless they are fighting with each
other, which frankly is their wasted energy. Caring doesn't mean
control or making other people happy. It means casting bread on
the water so that nourishment is possible, if not certain. My husband is an equal partner in the station wagon, the laundry, and the

dishes. If he weren't, the house would be filthier than it is. Women who don't have male partners in their house or male partners in their work, who instead have other "children" to take care of, are the ones who get in trouble caring. This problem is structural. It is a public problem. It is not a problem inherent in caring alone. When we learn to generalize that caring is good, but not when women have to do it alone, then we will spend less time worrying about the expense of caring.

Caring for a family or a public can't be done alone. It ceases to be caring if we are the only ones doing it. That kind of caring dwindles quickly to a form of self-abuse in which others are glad to participate.

So why am I going to shoot the next person who snidely advises me to take better care of myself? Why do I encourage other women to do the same? Why this long defensive description of the schedule and its many parts and partners? The reason is fairly simple. I feel like I am under attack. That women ministers with lots of energy are being shot at by some new and sinister form of do-goodism. Its name is *take care of yourself.* Its goal is to get women back under wraps, to keep us from having the fun of our own contributions to the world. We're doing too much and it is making lots of people uncomfortable. Unlike many male ministers, we have that second shift. We signed up for the double shift of life and work. We see family as an extension of ministry and ministry as an extension of family. Unlike many professionals in ministry, we don't change gears for the office and then back again at home. There is communion, not separation, between the several circles of our vocation. For most of us, children come absolutely first. They are the first circle. But we don't hoard our love for the world on behalf of our children. We make priorities instead. If these are our choices, and more often than not they are, they carry our authority. Rather than taking care of ourselves, women should be organizing partners in caring. Husbands, co-workers, children, street people, friends, in-laws, and neighbors. Rather than backing off our full schedules, I think we should be inviting other people to take part in them.

Of course, if our caring is a game we play with the purpose of getting other people's approval or fascination, then we have simply added a female step to the dance of the calendar and its busy, busy drumbeat. Not all men are busy in ungraceful ways, nor are all women busy gracefully: choosing a full life has the consequence of busyness. Caring is something that expands by its very nature. You can try to care well for a few things, and if you succeed, you will find more people calling your name. Welcome one homeless person to your congregation and see what happens. The head of a local welfare agency once told me that he didn't want to provide good service to his clients because doing that would only increase the demand. It is a very complex excuse for not caring.

When freely chosen, as part of a person's criteria for life, busyness is not all that bad. What is bad is assuming that all the caring that an institution or a family does has to come from Mom or minister. Caring goes wrong when one person carries all the responsibility for it. It can safely expand if it is done publicly, with invitations all over the place. It carries authority only to the degree that the caring person cares lightly, fully aware that he or she may fail at any minute to fully partner with the other or the matter. Yes, caring is individual and it is public. We care for the impersonal fabric of society as much as we care for the persons who nest in that fabric.

Of course, it would be better if the world were organized so all adults with or without children could work six hours a day outside the home and thus have some legitimate writing or gardening or praying time. But when that day comes, I'll be organizing the workers at the Susan B. Anthony Nursing Home or lamenting the decline in daughters or daughters-in-law. Right now I actively choose work and children and friends and quiet. I choose to have a full plate. That's how I take care of myself. Getting tired is a consequence of those choices. Getting tired means getting sick more often than is preferred. But to argue that I have to give up my full plate so I'd never be tired or sick, is just mean. It's a protection racket, a counter-defensive strike, a sideswipe at freedom. It is another way that the world fears the capacities of women and, fearful, puts us down.

Fatigue is not the sin it's cracked up to be by the self-care movement. Nor is weakness or sickness. Sin traditionally has been quite the opposite. It has been that morbid affair with the self that poisons public life. Sin has traditionally been understood as selfishness, and for the life of me, I can't figure out what "taking care of yourself" is if it's not selfishness. Does that mean that I encourage other people to walk over me or that sacrifice is my cup of tea? Of course not. I find my life in taking responsibility for my gifts and graces, in making the contributions I was meant to make to the world. One of my contributions will be the spirits that flow in my three children. Another will be what I do in my ministry. A third will be the abundance of my own spirit as it survives the difficulties that are set out for it. Separating these different spheres will not be easy. My life is just as important as these other lives. But it finds its importance in relationship with those lives, not alone at yoga class or at the hairdresser.

So, if you really want me to slow down and do less, if the chaos of my admittedly overbooked life is getting to you—or if you think

my contribution has become haggard or that I am just caring for
you because I want something in return—by all means ask me to
rest. I will appreciate your concern. Deeply. I don't want to look
like an overdeveloped suburb any more than you want to have to
look at another one. I want the plantings around my house to look
mature, I want space left over, I want unused space in my life. I
need margin as much as anything or anyone else does. If you think
I'm looking crowded, say so. But don't accuse me of "not taking
care of myself." That I simply don't plan to do. Fatigue is simply not
public enemy number one. Selfishness is. We women, especially
ministers, are going to need all the courage we can muster to exercise our authorities in energetic, caring directions. That we can care
well and long appears to make some people very uncomfortable.
We need to learn to be comfortable in other people's discomfort;
this comfort amidst discomfort requires the exercise of our authority.

Authority for women is frequently our power to care. When that
authority is sniped at and we are made to feel guilty for overdoing
our authority, nothing less than our ability to control ourselves is at
stake. We must guard ferociously our abilities to care. That sometimes means filling up our calendars and our plates to overflowing.
If and when it is by grace that this fullness occurs, authority flows.
If by guilt or imitation of clergy busyness, authority is blocked. How
do we know the difference? I don't really know. You can just feel it
by the absence of pain in the back of your neck or the presence of
a smile on your face as midnight nears. Authority contains its own
ability to measure itself, to know oneself well enough to discern the
limits, certainly, but also to see the possibilities. Yes, there are limits
to our capacities to care, but so few of us ever get to them that we
really don't know where they are. Genuine authority is shaking
hands with the possibilities for care that God has given us.

CHAPTER 21

Living Together:
The Authority of Hospitality

Lest the authority of caring seem too easy, too much of a sure thing for women or men, I offer a story to show that caring has to do with providing hospitality. I want to be sure that we understand hospitality and caring not as fixing things, but as living together.

Once upon a time, long ago and far away, there was an assistant pastor who was working very hard and a senior pastor who was working very hard in a very large and hardworking church. When they weren't tired from all that hard work, they fought about their job descriptions and their status relative to each other. The junior pastor felt that he did all the work and the senior pastor got all the money and status, so he went to the Board of Trustees and demanded a raise and a change in title. He didn't want to be an assistant pastor any more. He wanted to be an associate pastor.

The Board of Trustees, fresh from their own status wars in workplaces, laughed in his face. Son, they all but said, things are different here. We are a church. You have no right to demand a change in status, particularly one upwards. Read your Bible. It clearly says we are all to be servants.

The senior pastor said pretty much the same thing, although for entirely different reasons and at much greater length. He had also done his tour as an assistant pastor, and he did not want anything to pull, push, or shake him back down the ladder of success that he had so vigilantly climbed. Hell would freeze over, he informed the by now b-o-r-e-d of trustees, before he would lose an inch of his status relative to that hardworking but nevertheless theologically incorrect upstart.

For his conclusion, he too quoted the Bible. It clearly says we are all to be servants. Because preachers never say things just once, but rather many different times in different ways, this senior pastor, clutching his Bible in his right hand and his title in his left, gave a brief, but thorough, sermon on servanthood. It was already 11:15, the meeting having gone on a bit, and so the members took deep breaths and listened to what their pastor, excuse me, senior pastor, had to say on the subject.

Part one. *The last shall be first and the first shall be last.* A metaphysical and ontological treatise on numbers, status, position involving numerology and other ancient mysteries. Part two. *Be ye servants of one another.* A social and psychological treatise on how we are all one, yet many, many, yet one, ending in a rally call to *e pluribus unum* with special emphasis on servanthood and assorted footnotes on stewardship (stewardship being another one of those biblical words with etymological, if not philosophical, roots in the concept of servanthood). Part three. (Having trouble, folks? Don't worry. This guy is just getting started.) Now comes the practical part. Here he applies part one and two to what is normally called real life, but who can remember what real life is at this point, so long has the meeting gone on. Real life. Teamwork, he startles his dozing audience by announcing, is the true meaning of servanthood, which is why we are not giving this guy a raise or a change in title or status, but rather the opportunity for more servanthood. Let's let him assist at some of the larger funerals. Amen. The assistant pastor has to be restrained physically as he lunges for the senior pastor's throat. The meeting has peaked in more ways than one because Mrs. Peabody is now ready to speak.

I don't know if you have met Mrs. Peabody; she is a fictional character I have used before whenever I need a heroine to get the clergy out of their messes. She wears her hair in a bun. She reads her Bible. She makes a mean chocolate chip cookie. She has a perfect attendance pin at church cleanups. And she does not suffer fools gladly.

She begins to read from the fifteenth chapter of the Gospel of John. The serenity in her voice wakes the rest of the trustees up. She soothes them with the bold weariness of her own speech, implying that she joins Jesus in having seen all of this before, and that it impresses her less each time she has to see it. "Henceforth," she quotes Jesus as saying, "I do not call you servants, for the servant doesn't know what the Lord is doing. From now on I will call you friends."

Following her text, she makes her conclusion, which, of course, is to fire both pastors. She has made that suggestion before to no avail, and so she returns to the serenity of her own silence.

The trustees are too deeply entrenched in the mire of hierarchy and its oil slick of servanthood to implement her intelligent suggestion, and thus they call the meeting to an end and tell the pastors to fight it out in the morning. The assistant pastor demands a better office, one closer to the bathroom. The senior pastor refuses to be any closer to the assistant than he already is. The meeting limps to a close.

The next day, Jim, the head of the trustees, reviews his own experience at work in the light of this very dark meeting. He also has people above and below him who tell him with some precision who they are in the scheme of things. He also has made commitments in Sunday School to the notion of servanthood. He too wants very much to have a lot of status and to do a lot of good with it, just like the two pastors. The pastors are not alone in these confusions.

And that Mrs. Peabody is becoming nuttier by the minute. Hauling out that Bible verse at midnight is just like her. Last month she wanted to change the town's entire social service system. Something about giving the poor direct vouchers, rather than a lot of social workers. Let them decide their own way how to do things rather than servicing them all the time. She once again was up to her etymological tricks. Service, she said, has its root in the word servanthood. We should never try to help people, or wait on them, or serve them, she said. We should only try to be their friends. To give them hospitality. Again she played word games. Hospitality she said is the opposite of hostility. Latin roots, *hospes. Hostes.* To take hostage is hostile. To give hospice is hospitable. Open your hearts and homes to the poor and the dying and the troubled and the rest will follow, she said. All these services are wrong because we pay for them with money rather than with affection. Our authority as Christians, she said, is our ability to give hospitality. To open our hearts and doors, that's all. To be friends, not servants. That's all. There isn't enough time to do these things much less to waste it fighting about who gets paid the most to be the best servant. The social service people spend half the day in the same fight as our pastors. Who should get more because she gives more? It's disgusting. Imagine Mrs. Peabody using language that strong. Disgusting.

She went on to say that social services being all the rage, the gross national product actually grows if you have more sickness and more addiction and more poverty. Social workers have more things to fix that way. They get to have more employees in their agency and when they climb up to boss level, their status improves. She was really ranting and raving by the time that meeting ended, wanting to change the whole basis on which the world operates. Jesus insults the Pharisees, she insults the social workers. They're just trying to do their job and to be good, decent, servant-type people. Imagine. It was really the same argument she used years ago when she antagonized half of the women's fellowship by saying they shouldn't send clothes to Church World Service, but instead send money so that local industries that made clothes could develop in these various countries. She said you have to help smart or something like that. Imagine that, offending the good ladies of the women's fellowship.

Jim almost never thought about religion. He usually spent most of his time thinking about how much he'd like to move into an outer office. From there he was sure the situation at work would improve. The number of donations would surely increase if he were in charge of collections. He happened to work for the Muscular Dystrophy Society. The woman now in charge was almost as stupid as his secretary. If he had something other than incompetents above and below him, imagine what he could do.

Anyway in the middle of all these drowsy muses, he decided to give Mrs. Peabody a call. Take her out to lunch. Help her out with her loneliness a bit. Maybe that would get her off those various brooms she was riding. She'd probably get a lift just hearing from him.

When they had lunch, Mrs. Peabody had already forgotten about the war between the pastors. She didn't even mention Church World Service. Instead she focused a kind of remarkable attention on him. "Jim, are you happy? Do you feel fulfilled? How are the children really doing in school? Your wife, is she satisfied with what she is doing? On whom do you rely, Jim? What's really important in your life? Do you feel caught anywhere?"

Jim, fighting back the tears so unused to such direct concern was he, finally burst out, "Oh, yes, Mrs. Peabody, I really need help. I'm really not very satisfied at all. Can you help me?" She shook her head no. "No?" he gasped. "No, you won't help me?" She said, "Of course not, I don't help anybody. I don't believe in helping. I believe in friendship. In standing close to each other and getting through tight places with other people as a kind of companion. It's the same way I feel about servanthood, Jim. I don't want to be anybody's servant. And I don't want anybody to be my servant. But I will be a friend if I can. I can offer hospitality. And I want it offered back to me."

"But, Mrs. Peabody, don't you get hurt a lot? Don't friends just take you and use you? Don't you remember that guy you let stay in the church and then he stole some stuff from us? You remember, that black guy..."

She interrupted him. "What difference does it make that he was black? He could have been white and still taken stuff from us. Jim, you have to be very careful about using color words. If you need to use them, then talk about the white guy who was the last guy to give us a hard time at the church when we tried to offer him hospitality. Giving hospitality means that you may get taken every now and then, and if you don't understand that, then you don't understand why Jesus was taken straight to the cross, and if you don't understand that, well, I can't imagine how this congregation was foolish enough to put you on the Board of Trustees. . ."

OK. OK. Jim was feeling that old prickly Mrs. Peabody whom everybody knew so well. So, she continued. "Jim, what do you need and how can I help you to get it?"

"Why would you be willing to do that for me?" Jim just had to know. "Simple," she responded. "I'm not doing it for you, I'm doing it for God. God wants us to be committed to each other the way God is committed to us. That's the meaning of that big word covenant. We are to be committed to each other the way God is committed to us. Willing and ready to be taken, if necessary. Providing the hospitality of friendship, freely, as slaves to no one, not even God. . ." She stopped herself then because she knew she was starting to sound preachy. Mrs. Peabody lived a kind of low overhead life. Not much status to protect, only friendship to offer. Her tea she steeped well. Her experience she sifted. Her gospel she tried to understand. She carried the authority of hospitality, and she carried it well. She had worked beside so many people for so long that in her you saw the beauty of shovels, rakes, brooms, and rags. She was a good companion in the labors of life. She would make a good pastor or assistant pastor or associate pastor and, believe me, she wouldn't really care which. Frankly, I'd just like to have her as my friend.

Mrs. Peabody has more authority than she needs. She knows how to walk a piece of the journey with trustees and with the Jims of the world and with the poor. She knows how to leave them alone on their path when that time comes. She knows how to care in public and in private and she doesn't have to change her clothes or her pearls or her way of thinking when she shifts from one site to another. Hospitality is her authority.

CHAPTER 22

Humoring:
A Blessing from a Curse

Any woman who cannot find humor in her situation will be a stranger to authority. We are the epitome of what makes humor work. We are the resident *other* in Western culture. We are the opposite of all that is normal. We are aliens, strangers, the permanent *ex matriates*. If people are free enough to laugh at the surprises in their lives, if they show up at Aunt Susie's funeral and discover the officiant to be the opposite of what they thought he would be, we can be instantly amusing. What is not funny, of course, is the way people have of excluding surprises from their lives. They like to control things. Humor is the best way I know to put up with the fact that you can't.

When women adopt the internal attitude of humor, that marvelous attitude that Friedman calls a non-anxious presence, we become free not to care so much about hurts. The hurts will keep coming, but we do not have to continue to be hurt by them. In our preparation for them, we get a bit of release. Another good expression for this attitude is metaphysical nonchalance; it is important not to care about hurtful things. Because none of us is really capable of doing that, we may as well laugh at them, or try to, or develop the posture of Friedmanian nonchalance. It will at least confuse our enemies.

I find that the best way to develop our natural humor is to bless and to curse a lot. Tevye in "Fiddler on the Roof" sang to God. We can keep a running commentary going heavenward if blessing and cursing become our primary verbs.

Thus, I have started a national search for new expletives. There is a certain word that begins with *F* that I am sick of hearing. There's another word that begins with *S* that I am sick of hearing. I still sort of like the word that begins with *B* and includes the word that begins with *S*. That's to show you that I am not a stick-in-the-mud or a candidate for a new kind of women's temperance union.

I like the *B-S* word because it describes so much so fully. But the adjectives that begin with *F* and end with *ing* or begin with *S* and end with *Y* are just plain boring. People just aren't showing enough imagination with their expletives, and that's why I have launched a new national contest. It is the How to Express Dismay Without Using the Words That Begin with *F* and *S* First National Competition. The rules are simple.

To win this contest the new expletive must express dismay without demeaning the human body or its functions. It must be repeatable by children in the presence of grandparents. It must sound good when pronounced in a disgusted tone of voice. Women clergy must be able to use it in a public setting. Things like *gosh* and *darn, gee whiz* or *heavens to betsy* won't be considered for historical reasons. Frankly, they too are a bit overused. *Damn* suffers a similar fate, although expletives with theological content, such as *God* and *damn, for heavens sake, holy smoke* and the like will be considered if fresh combinations are presented. Juvenile expressions like *whillikers* and *holy moly* can be considered, but to win this contest, the expression should have an adult flavor. *Folderal* is a good, if Victorian, example. Phrases are okay but hard to get out in the white heat of disgust. For example, saying that Ronald Reagan gave one the *jim jams* is okay but not qualified for contest entry due to its complexity. Being *P-Oed* at him doesn't qualify under rule number one regarding the body. Calling up images of garbage or waste will run risks of repeating the word that begins with *S,* which concept we are trying to eliminate, if you know what I mean, so don't bother snooping around in the dump heap for a winner.

Stick to more inert channels of thought. The committee meeting is still on the first item of the agenda and your husband is going to work right now, leaving three children at home in the toaster oven for safe keeping. Your husband is looking (again) for a lost shirt while the head of your Board of Trustees is trying to tell you why he lost the keys to the boiler room (again). The daughter of the deceased has just informed you as politelty as possible that her mother would not have wanted a woman to conduct her funeral.

Consider the moments when expletives are necessary and surely you'll think of something good. Consider the former minister of your congregation. He/she is always a jerk (deeply troubled person is the pastoral code) or at least good for a jerk joke. Consider traffic jams. Or looking for a parking space and being sideswiped on the way into it. Consider being behind a sleeper when the light turns green. These are the moments when expletives take on meaning.

Think of dropping a ten-pound bag of potatoes on your foot. Or
losing the car keys. Consider what the bank is making on your
mortgage or how much you paid for the last stove you had to return. Live into the experience of the expletive. Avoid moral categories that slyly put you down for expressing dismay. After all, everyone gets *P-Oed* once in awhile. You might consider interfacing with
a significant other. Group entries are permissible as are multiple
ideas. All entries must be received by April Fool's Day. Winners of
the contest will be announced in local church bulletins.

Low-cost forms of personal entertainment are absolutely necessary to people in ministry. When we've completed the contest for
best curse, we'll start a contest for best blessing. It may not be as
funny, but it is just as much fun. We will have to shift gears, just as
we do day by day when even humor won't ameliorate all our hurt.
If cursing doesn't work, we will have to wrestle the hurt for a
blessing.

Whenever we are forced to look for the places of blessing in our
lives, we necessarily travel outside ourselves. We may have found
the authority of our own voice and our own language. We may have
found authority in hospitality and the ability to care. There may
even be authority in our secrets. But we will need blessings to realize these authorities. The ability to control ourselves is necessary,
and blessing is always done in relationship. Family and friends either bless us or don't bless us with all sorts of possibilities in between. They either confirm the authority of our voice, caring, and
hospitality or they don't. Some of the deepest hurt—and greatest
blessing—is at the place where we are not confirmed even after we
have found our own criteria.

God blesses what we cannot. Such grace is beyond our control,
but the giving and receiving of it is not. Sometimes the control may
be to gain the capacity to live without blessing while remaining
open to its possibility. Other times the discipline is to receive from
others whatever minimum confirmation they are able to give.
Whichever, the search for blessing amidst the cursing never ceases.
It is an attitude of expecting to be happy, of expecting to be met on
the road, of relinquishing past hurts even as they turn into load-
bearing resentments.

Letting water run off our backs is a preparation for blessing. My
friend inspires me in this. She has been abused by her church system. She has been severely disappointed by her husband. Her father was an alcoholic. The package is lethal. Her church, which is
supposed to take care of its own, doesn't, and now she is an associate in a large congregation after having pastored some interesting
spots by herself. It would be easy for her to be mowed down by

these experiences of male power wrongly used. Like the blades of grass taken swiftly, inevitably, and frequently by power mowers, she is typical. Typical of a kind of woman whose frustration pots boils over into either depression or alcoholism or just the vague, hazy wandering of a prematurely has-been life. Her only chance at beating these realities is to fight them for their blessing in endurance.

My friend's realities deserve the laugh of God. We must oppose them with God's opposition. They are not godly. Their power is all puffery. That means laughing at them, cursing them as creatively as possible and as long as necessary, and moving on. It means letting them go, confident of God's victory down the road. We let them go so that we can move on down the road, open to blessing.

The true victim is the one who closes down to blessing. Despair is as much a sin as the wrong and violent use of power. The limits of trouble are determined by the troubled themselves.

Sometimes, because so much trouble has already happened, we start enjoying the old trouble in a sick kind of way or we fear the new trouble just up the road. We waste not just time but also life in worrying, in fondling old hurts, in predicting new ones. Some of these patterns are so lethal that they actually become funny themselves. A man called a friend to tell him that his car had broken down and he wouldn't be able to make a very important meeting. The friend's reply to the tale of woe was predictable: *Don't worry. I'm Jewish. I don't expect cars to work.*

Blessing is possible when humor is our guide. Humor takes on the logic of trouble; it lets it go and then challenges its right to determine future reality.

On our fifth anniversary, my husband said with utter delight, "Do you realize that nothing, absolutely nothing, has turned out the way we thought it would?" My response should have been, "Of course, that's how it always is." Instead, I was deeply moved by the openness of reality, by its baseline in humor and astonishment.

CHAPTER 23

How Are We Doing with Our Authority? Some Afterthoughts

We have looked at five areas to discover sources of women's authority. One is the use of our own language; another is our ability to care; a third is our capacity for hospitality. Our secrets brought to speech and the common sense of our humor also give us criteria by which to judge ourselves. Were these criteria allowed to shape our hope for ourselves and our ministry, authority would be an entirely different matter for us than it is now.

Each of these criteria came into view as I thought about how women already have and use authority. They are not shoulds so much as givens. The process of developing authority for women is turning these givens into shoulds, these received gifts into objectives that require nurturing, deepening, and certainly criticism.

My mentor in community organizing, Saul Alinski, would describe my method as turning the worst negative (our maligned femininity) into our greatest asset. You think I'm emotional? You ain't seen nothing yet. Communities, Alinski argues, change by these kinds of strategic, objectifying decisions. Communities change power structures when they can target the head of the local welfare office and expose him as an SOB. Yes, the male language of "target" is intended here. There is a two-way street. In the world most of us want to live in, we can describe realities differently; each of us can become multilingual. There is almost nothing about Alinski that is female or even that valued femininity; but I can take his reality and his gifts, spoken in the male voice, to help me understand my reality.

There are women who find borrowing strategic targeting from male tradition offensive; I respect their perspective. As black people have had to struggle with the issues of integration and separation, so have and will women. I am an integrationist. There are other legitimate options.

To target our presumed weaknesses as categories of potential strength is to exercise agency, not communion. It is to act on our own behalf in a strategic way. It is to rename the world inside us a spiritual act and that outside us a political act. To position caring against productivity as a matter of authority, to take just one example, has to be a political act as well as a spiritual act. Both the public and the private levels are involved simultaneously. Which comes first, the authority to care from your soul or the authority to care from the society? The answer always has to be both. The chicken or the egg? Rearranging the furniture inside us won't help at all unless we can rearrange some of the furniture in the local welfare office as well. It is part of our depth as public ministers that we understand the simultaneous nature of the process of change, both inside and outside, all at once.

The criteria I have posed as potential authorities for women become a good basis for self-evaluation, even for job descriptions in ministry. Are we using our own voice to describe reality as we see and experience it or are our voices borrowed? Who are we kidding with these borrowed voices? What will it take for us to find our own voice? Which communities can help us? Which will get in the way? How do we change our lives so that we spend more time in helpful places and less living among the obstacles? Given the trouble using our own voice will cause us, how will we manage the pain?

As people who judge ourselves by our capacities to care and to include the strange and the stranger, how are we doing? This culture pounds these capacities out of people at every turn. Don't overdo it. Be careful. Care only about number one and number one's friends. Don't give strangers a ride. It is a hostile not hospitable culture dependent on the ascendancy of agency over communion at every turn. How can we navigate this culture in such a way that we escape its messages, but do not lose our capacities to care and give hospitality?

As clergy, how do we leave communities more capable than when we arrived? Does our association with the homeless or with young people leave them stronger or weaker? I think of leadership as that process of being very active and then releasing responsibility, as letting go and actually rendering oneself useless over time. Like Mrs. Peabody, we need to walk our piece of the road with others well, and then we need to get off. It is a mark of authority that the communities that we gather and that are already gathered are stronger when we leave than when we arrived. As people who judge ourselves by our willingness to protect and possibly expose secrets and who develop over time the ability to tell the difference,

how are we doing? Are there things we know that we should be
telling? Are there things we don't know that we should find out,
about ourselves or our community or our loved ones? Do we have
things to say to cruel fathers, obnoxious husbands, unjust bishops?
Would the speaking of these secret feelings, either privately or publicly and collectively, not create the kind of borders that our care
needs to remain strong? Are we keeping secrets from ourselves?
How well exercised are our verbs, our curses, and our blessings?
How well exercised are our humors? Have we moved into the
house of tragedy and given the power away to man and mammon
to determine our days? Or have we opened to the confidence of
manna and thus greet our days with a sense of possibility, sure of a
good laugh even if we have to create it ourselves?

In all these criteria, voice, care, hospitality, secrets, and humor, I
am assuming an ongoing, critical process. Women must be very
careful that when their gifts become criteria they are not privatized,
but rather kept public and covenantal as expressions of God's will
for the "ancient city." They are not just for our networks or parishes
or friends or family. They are not *not* private; it is just that they are
public at the same time. Again, we see the two-way street. We participate with other women in the development of our voice: listening
is as important as is speaking. The ideal criteria is both a collective
voice and an individual voice. Caregiving and hospitality are two
sides of the same coin; one is the capacity to care for those we
know, the other is the capacity to care for who and what we don't
know.

Humor is a wager that in the power struggle between God and
mammon, God is going to win. Tragedy bets on the other side:
*mammon has already won; perhaps God is even an accessory. De-
spair 10, hope 0. The game is over.* But we know better.

Secrets are disclosed internally and externally. We hide as much
from ourselves as the world hides from itself. The ongoing process
of naming and connecting our personal and our public realities is
the methodology women now use, somewhat intuitively. I am suggesting that we go beyond intuition and make it more consciously
and objectively our own.

Feminists frequently name this method that of the both/and. Earlier it was referred to as the personal being the political and the
political being the personal. There is authority in the ability to walk
back and forth on the two-way street. Consciousness about that walk
enhances the authority; the greater our consciousness of where we
are and what we are doing at any given stop on the street, the
greater the authority, the greater the opportunity to take responsi-

bility for ourselves and our position, thereby encouraging others to do the same.

There is nothing keeping men from walking this two-way street, too.

I think of this responsibility-taking as adult caring. Women have been developmentally stuck for a long time in taking care of others as though they were our children. We have overdone it and made fairly much of a mess of it. I don't think that anyone would say that children raised by women who lived through and for them were done any favor. Nor would the men and the women clergy who have done everything for their parishes find many fans. Community organizers who manipulate and social workers who "help" make a similar mistake: they mother instead of befriending. The people who have developed their own authority in such a way as to encourage others to develop as well are the nurturers who are respected. They are mature, unstuck developmentally in parent/child formulas for leadership. Why else would we seek authority except to earn respect? How else can we earn respect save by deserving it? That means an ability to control ourselves so that others may control themselves. Authority is controlling ourselves, period. Authority does not have the goal of getting others to control themselves. It is simply self-control because that is what an adult does. If others take that responsibility for themselves as well, so much the better. As the Gospel says elsewhere, there are a lot of things we can have by not heading straight for them.

PART V

Conclusion

CHAPTER 24

Deepening the Contradictions

In this book I have tried to restring some pearls, to use common sense to repair notions of ministry. I wanted to understand what women mean when we—some of us, some of the time—talk about security and power and authority. I wanted to understand how women could find security in a world where communion and connection are discounted. I wanted to understand what kind of power we need to do our jobs as ordained ministers. I wanted to disclose the authority we now have and to make it a more conscious feature of our lives and ministries.

On the matter of security I came to terms with a little secret: even mowing the lawn is not a simple matter for women. We get involved in the relationships, and once that happens, we are less than secure. Men tend not to be nearly as interested in matters of relationship as we are. More money or more status, even more hard work, will not increase our security. We can be safe, but not using the strategies we have up to now. We don't need to become *less* open to connection or communion or relationships, but more so. An open invitation for men to join us in communion, as we have joined them in agency, will create a two-way street in ministry. That might make us, and the world, more safe.

On the matter of power I worked from a story of losing my lane to a truck driver. Again, the two-way street became a hopeful strategy. I had to confess to some serious sour grapes in the ministry and concede that repentance was the road to power. I had to repent, but I also needed to be a part of a community of repentance. Repentance is the concrete action that follows on the heels of the experience of forgiveness. Thus in stringing the pearls of power, I had to think of actions clergy could take once we have dedicated ourselves to opening more lanes in ministry. I talked about job descriptions and what to do if a parish began to disagree with itself

about something important. I pictured us living outside of the fishbowl, among our people, as forgiven leaders who have not aban-
doned the power we need to make our way, but rather have refined
it and spread it around. I was not talking to women only. I couldn't
really think of anything that applied only to us alone. No doubt that
is yet more evidence of my inability to mow my lawn all by myself.

On the matter of authority, I talked about the experience of trying to raise my children. I became more deeply aware of how society has given me a little permission to raise my daughter as a boy,
but not my sons as girls. This lack of respect for the authority of the
feminine becomes a genuine barrier to women in the doing of
ministry. Men also face it but they don't see it everywhere they look.
I hoped we would find the courage to let the feminine surface. In
hospitality and caring, in using our voices and telling our secrets, in
an awareness of the constant flow of blessing and curse in our lives,
women (and men) can make friends with the authorities of the
feminine.

I don't claim to have restrung my pearls in an orderly way. I've
not been led along a completely rational pathway. I've simply
walked a few more steps toward understanding what women have
meant to ministry, besides the placing of darts in the vestments. We
have given the church a chance to become androgynous, and that is
helping ministry in the Protestant churches become more public
and more full. These preferences for the public in ministry and the
androgynous in gender roles are still a minority point of view in
Protestantism. I can only repeat my deep difficulty with the majority
and the mainstream. Unlike Mark Twain, who enjoyed piloting his
steam boat right to the bitter end of its time, I am alienated from
much of my role in the church right now. I see the railroads coming to put us out of business and wonder why we are resisting
them. In other words, my commitment to the current institution is
less than serious. I think many women join me in being committed
to a kind of ministry that is not yet formed. We love the church, but
it is a church that is yet to be. We are out of the fishbowl on our
own. Last I heard there was no sin in living in hope, actively waiting
for a realized eschatology.

Many studies are now confirming that women seem to be leaving the ministry when they get close to fifty years of age. Many of
my friends are very close to the door. So far the explanations for
this behavior (which repeats the pattern of the last century when
women were ordained in larger numbers after the Civil War) are
sociological: the glass ceiling on salary and status drive women to
other careers at mid-life. But I think there are other reasons and

they are spiritual. We can't always mow our lawn our own way; we can't always hold our lane in traffic; and we can't raise our children in the way our intuitions tell us is right. There is insufficient security, insufficient power, and insufficient authority for women in ministry. We get tired of representing communion in the world of ecclesiastical agency. We love the ministry, but are not yet sure that it loves us. That a secular job will not satisfy our hunger to be normal doesn't matter. We can't be blamed for looking.

The androgyny that women bring the church has at least three purposes. One is to replace the model of the corporation or the clinic with that of the open family (I do not mean nuclear family; I mean familial relationship). The church, in its exaggerated masculinity, has become like a corporation with ministers modeling after managers and hierarchy the dominant organizational mode. I'm not sure this model has been useful to the people of God. Maybe it was at one time, but not in my recent experience. Mixed in with the corporate model of minister as Chief Executive Officer is that of the minister as private therapist. We heal people one by one, doors closed to our offices, medical model blaring out its presumed wisdom. In the family the minister is a mother, father, sister, or brother. The organization is much more chaotic with the goal being growing up and becoming whole. (Yes, I know there are sick models for family where the goal is to keep the children young and the parents in charge.)

Evelyn Newman was about to be installed as the first associate for pastoral services at Riverside Church in New York. She wanted her children to accompany her in the procession at the installation service to demonstrate her belief that the activity of ministry was an extension of the activity in family. Newman has a theory of concentric circles, with blood family always being the most important and ministry extending outward from family to the larger world. It has a biblical ring. At any rate, the installation committee authorized her children to walk down the aisle with her. Then at the last minute, Evelyn was told this was not appropriate. Two ministry models were clashing: with one, we walk down the aisle alone to do it alone; with the other we walk in with a crowd. Evelyn refused solo passage: "Then you'll have to find another minister to install." Another lane was opened up, and Evelyn was installed with her children at her side. Now, she reports, many people include their families in their installation services.

When and as women enter the ministry, not as aliens but bringing the authority of our peculiar contributions and capacities with us, we will change the management and therapeutic models into something different. Hierarchy has already been dealt many blows simply by our being there in ministry, "relating" more than "mowing." We have democratized many tables already.

I met a Rabbi at a meeting recently. While engaging in small talk, I happened to tell her a story about my children and their dresser drawers. My four-year-old daughter was with me. I told the Rabbi that Katie had been picking out colors to paint her dresser. Then I reported how I had painted my sons' dressers a blue-green color because blue was Isaac's favorite color and green Jacob's favorite color. The boys had raised a holy fit: "Why are you painting *our* dressers with *your* colors?" I assumed I would find some sympathy from my new friend because she was the mother of three. Instead she said, "Well, why *were* you painting their dressers with your colors?" We hadn't known each other for two minutes, but her response delighted me. Finally to find someone with the authority of communion so deep in her that she couldn't even violate it for small talk or small people. Someone who lived according to participatory democracy in her bones. Someone who thought the unusual was usual. Had I told this story to a man, or to a woman who thinks like a man, I would have gotten the sympathy I wanted. Kids, aren't they terrible, always wanting to make their own decisions and fly their own colors.

Shohama—her name comes from Genesis and means at least the onyx of wisdom—showed me one of the things androgyny in ministry would mean. It would mean the normalizing of democratic and communal forms and the abnormalizing of managerial and therapeutic hierarchies and authorities. It would mean raising our parishes as well as we try to raise our children. It would mean a process of putting maturity on the table as our goal. Neither management nor therapy has maturity as its destination; in fact both contain inner resistances to democratic maturity. Wellness is more the goal of therapy, and even in these enlightened days, wellness still involves too much adjustment to the status quo. Orderly growth is more the goal of management. The models themselves undermine the more feminine authorities.

There is at least one more thing that women may bring to ministry. We are already shifting ministry into more of a relational model. We are resisting hierarchical forms in favor of democratic authorities and maturities. We will also deepen other contradictions to combine the things that others say won't combine. We will bring our methodology of both/and, not either/or. Just as the family model predicts a weakening of hierarchy, this method opens up a lane where potentially contradictory, or at least different, things may happen at once.

Evelyn Newman shows concretely that family is a model for ministry that we may dare to explore as a route to security and power and authority. Shohama assures me that we don't have to be in charge all the time, that it is both safe to share authority and power, and desirable, useful, good. I am learning (slowly) to be less afraid of the contradictions between my power and your power, my authority and yours. Sometimes I can even be glad because contradictions may contain promise. I have grown through these disorderly troubles. Order has never been so helpful.

Imagine that a distraught friend phones you one evening right after you have put your slippers on. You tell her, yes, I'll be right over. According to Doctor Bernie Siegel of *Love, Medicine and Miracles* fame, you will probably be a victim of cancer. If you answer no to your friend, your life insurance premium just went down. It is so refreshing to finally have an accountant for our morality. Even if I misunderstood Dr. Siegel's more complex answer, which I probably did, still the common misreading presents an interesting dilemma: Live for others, we die ourselves. Golden rules never mention payment; they only pronounce.

The phone call that requests women nurturing is almost unrefusable. We have made an ideology out of nurture, so much so that there are days when I never want to hear the word again. I once heard a woman give a sermon at Union Seminary and nearly collapsed under the weight of her self-assurance about the importance of nurturing. She made it sound so easy. She seemed to consider herself fully capable of it at all times. I wondered which planet she lived on. I hoped she would stop taking so many feminist theology courses. I will enjoy the newer models of ministry more when motherhood receives the same critical approach that management and therapy now receive.

Carol LeMasters says there's a pervasive understanding among women that we are "more nurturing."[1] Thus when a phone call comes from a distraught friend and we feel like staying glued to our slippers, we have little permission. We are too nurturing for such comfort.

I wake every day at 6 a.m. to experience an hour of quiet before my children wake up to make, among other things, noise. It is then that I write and then that my maximum satisfaction is realized. Life alone is, predictably, an improvement over life together. Together I have to interact morally. Alone I can fantasize what I might do if so called upon and all my fantasies can evolve out of my best self. (My children also prefer videotapes to actual interaction.) In these fantasies, I bargain. I read each a story after cuddling them as they awake, even if it is closer to six than seven when I hear their warm

pajamas rustle down the hall, closing in on my word processor.
When the story is over, and the cuddles' warmth still remembered,
they seize on a toy or a project of their own and I return to write,
thus experiencing the both/and of agency and communion. We
compromise and everyone is happy.

My moral accountant, however, documents a different story. I
don't even have the coffee assisting me when pajamas rustle. I be-
grudge the story and the hug, but do it anyway out of my unruled
self. Motherhood, like ministry, is an archaeology of obligation.
Then I sneak away to the word processor, followed by three complaining elves none of whom can occupy themselves for a minute.
Before the sun has risen, I am angry. I am conflicted. Bernie Siegel
would say that I am trying to catch cancer. I would say that I was
just trying to write.

If I give the children all the morning time, I would never get to
write because I have to work for money the rest of the day. If I give
my friends all the evening time, I would never get to rest. But if I
don't give the children morning time, they don't get to school; they
don't have a mother who enjoys eating breakfast with them, we
don't have fun as a family or, if not fun, at least the repeating interaction over the lunchboxes that teaches us what living is. (Yes, my
husband is working away in this little drama, too. He is not reading
the paper. It takes fully two of us once the full-tilt boogie begins.)
Likewise if I don't take care of my friends, they won't take care of
me. We won't have any good laughs, or good mirrors, or good
springboards. There are costs to not having friends or children and
there are costs to having them. The contradictions deepen without
any assistance from me.

Cancer doesn't have to be a metaphor, but it can be. It is uncon-
trolled growth. It is *yes* to every cell. My normal strategy for dealing
with the frequent contradictions of daily living as a woman in family
and in ministry is cancerous: it is that old warhorse, the both/and.
Fully nurture others and fully nurture yourself. Say yes to every
phone call and yes to every cherub's cry, and religiously, absolutely
walk an hour a day and write an hour a day. Steal two hours for
yourself. I enjoy these 26-hour days when they happen, which is
once a week or so, just often enough to keep me hounding them.
But the number of things that can happen to disallow them is
downright amazing. The telephone is the number one offender. I'm
on my way out the door and pick it up only to hear a whingdinger.
Of course, the phone answering machine could pick it up and usually does, but then, say I, I still have to return the call later. Put up
with it now. Or I can see the full hour streaming before me for the
walk and decide that it's a great time to bake a cake. Just get it

started before you go. Or even more interesting, I call a friend. Do you want to go for a walk? She thinks I am distraught, or I really am distraught, but don't know it yet and am just using the walk as a disguise, and then she decides to come but she can't come till later when the children are back home. The possibilities for internal conflict are endless.

I've been meaning to ask Bernie Siegel about why his examples are so personal. I experience the distraught public as phoning me on a daily basis. A latchkey child is playing with matches. A teacher just growled at another because she has too many children in her class. People are lost in traffic on their way to the landfill. Their fumes are blowing smoke in the face of God; their garbage is piling on top of Mother Earth's head. The old ladies in the nursing homes are still waiting for a call from me. While these things are occurring, the men in charge of the government are voting against chemical weapons one day in the Senate and then becoming presidents and making speeches against them the next day. They use our safety to elect themselves. We are not safe with them. How dare I refuse these phone calls? My refusal will guarantee more cancer for everybody unless the children die young of drugs or war or something else my solitude will have refused to prevent.

The destination of my ministry is power in community to make justice, to stop these insults to God and to start the institutionalization of love. I use community to prevent trouble. The destination of my ministry is finding and exercising my peculiar authority as an individual and as a woman, finding and using my own voice, placing my gifts on a particular altar. I need and want to be safe while I do these things. My power depends on my ability to forgive myself for my own frequent failures in these matters and my ability to forgive the world's injustice and broken community. Without rest and care of my self, I lose the power of forgiveness and grace to the power of anger and fatigue. The authority of my particular capacity becomes one long useless effort.

My strategy for the 26-hour day won't work. It won't work because I am not a god, just a woman able to manage only twice that of a normal human being. I get too tired after a both/and day—or life. Maybe cancer is also a consequence; that I don't know yet. It is just something I get to worry about.

I have another strategy simmering. It is to actively deepen the contradictions. Passively allowing myself to be chased by contradictions, and with effort, adding hours to the day is futile. Instead I realize several times a day, I am doing what I want. What I choose is this conflict of both *me* and *us,* of living as deeply in it as possible. Of course, my writing is in conflict with my mothering. Both want my all, and neither can have it. Of course my ministry is in conflict with my writing, which is in conflict with my mothering. You can rearrange that sentence any way you want. Of course, my friends' needs are in conflict with my own. Both of us want the full undivided attention of the other, and neither of us can have that. Of course, the safety of the world is my safety. Of course, I have obligations to children whose names I don't know as well as to Isaac, Katie, and Jacob. How else could we live as one among many without all this cell dividing? Thus I choose to live a life of divided and dividing cells; it is not something I need fear. My choice is a full boat of conflict and contradiction, with some old life dying so that new might be born perpetually. To choose to live by a golden rule is different than passively accepting the difficulties of such a life. It is a choice that allows us to live securely amid all this insecurity.

On what basis did I or anyone else ever think it might be different? What absurd promises of order has reason made? Contradiction describes reality more accurately than harmony or order ever will. False harmony is the kind of place in which cancer has more opportunities, it seems to me. Deep contradictions, well understood, baptize the reality in which most of us already live.

Women's excluded hands bring to ministry a chance to change its shape. To stay off the large-scale and to value the small-scale. To become more like a family and less like an organization. To become less a place where some people are on top of each other in an orderly repression. To be less a place where everyone knows their place and stays in it and more a place where blue-green dressers hang open with unmended blue jeans dripping out. Even the blue jeans don't stay in their place and have to spend all day overhearing a conversation between a mother and a son about repainting what's already been painted.

The two-way street is not mess over order, or even community over hierarchy. It is not family as an unalloyed good and corporation as an unallowed evil. It is both this and that, living in some sort of disharmony harmoniously It is simple common sense. The conversation is open, shifting, changing; likewise the power. When both men and women walk a two-way street in ministry, both security and insecurity, power and powerlessness are legitimately present. People can see them at the table, talk about them, and sometimes even change them to the security of a more shared power.

NOTE

1. Carol LeMasters, "Unhealthy Uniformities" in *The Women's Review of Books,* October 1989.

Job Descriptions as Though the Gospel Is True

Author's Note: *This first appeared in the November/December 1989 issue of* Action Information *published by The Alban Institute. I think it gets at the heart of what I believe about ministry.*

If it is true that there is a new church promised by the Gospel, one just over the horizon, reachable by faithful journey, then new job descriptions are in order. We live as if the Gospel promise were true and our behavior changes in response to this wager.

Many practices in the church quickly require a new look. The oppositions at budget time between the pastor's salary and the mission budget prove flimsy. If the pastor is doing his or her job, it should be mission, not maintenance. Most pastors experience long dark nights of the soul in conflict between their own rising electric bills and their knowledge that many are getting ulcers worrying about when they will be turned off and where they will get the money to be turned back on. Don't worry, the electric company knows how to stay clear of such dark nights of the soul. They just charge for the extra service of on and off. But pastors (sometimes) live in a different economics. We are as worried about our own well being as any one, but we are too familiar with the gospel's priorities not to worry about others as well. Thus the false opposition between our salary and mission. Because this opposition is annual, it might make sense to reconsider the job description of the pastor. What if it was assumed by the congregation that half of their pastor's time—and therefore half of their salary—was a debt being paid to the poor? What if, instead of the pastor being the property of the parishioners, in that ancient selfishness where pastors are more like kept women than anything else, we assumed the pastor belonged to the community? That he or she was a gift freely given to the community in its task of restoring its streets? Wouldn't that change the balance in the budget from a niggling 8 or 9 percent to mission in the average congregation? Wouldn't it be evidence of changed hearts as well?

Likewise if a pastor made it his or her business to rest well, a community would be encouraged in the same practices. As long as the pastor joins the competitions of "busier than thou," the congregation can't really be expected to find grace. They'll be able to find lots of work at church, as too many already do, and little rest. The church still has a shot at being a sanctuary from the bile of an overly active society. But we lose that chance to the extent that pastors have the fullest date books, the weediest gardens, the rustiest cross country skis, and the highest blood pressure. The competitions need to reverse field: the prize going to the most well rested. An ancient sage, Seraph, I think, put it this way: "Find peace, and others will follow you anywhere."

Finally, we must consider where the responsibility for the new church and for Gospel journeying really lies. It does not lie with the pastor or with the church bureaucrats at headquarters. The responsibility belongs to the people who own the church. If people can't own the task of fulfilling their spiritual lives, then pastors can't begin to help them. That means that if you "don't like" the pastor, the options are to a) go elsewhere, b) start a new church, or c) have it out on the premises with the pastor and others. Dropping out, as though you weren't going to that restaurant any more because you don't like the food, is a spiritual cop out. It is soul lazy. The fact that too many pastors allow themselves to pick up these dropped responsibilities and to worry about declining church memberships is evidence of a victory for lay people, a slimy little victory but a victory nonetheless. Doctors aren't responsible for our health; cops aren't responsible for safe streets; politicians aren't responsible for cleaning up pollution; lawyers aren't responsible for solving conflicts between people; and pastors aren't responsible for souls. Pastors have enough trouble being responsible for their own souls without being responsible for the souls of people who don't care enough to bother about their own. This reversed assumption about responsibility lightens the load too many pastors carry. The lighter the load, the stronger the faith, the greater the capacity the faith has for getting down to the real work of ministry, which is nourishing those who are traveling towards God, keeping them fit and well fed, so that they may restore the streets to dwell in through their factories, offices, and kitchens.

As soon as we who pastor get out of the way of those who minister, as soon as they take the power back to care for each other, to counsel each other, to speak the word of God to each other, as soon as that reversal of power occurs, land will return to the land-less. People will own their own walk towards God and pastors will enjoy a new job description, one led more by the Gospel than by the social expectations that prevail.

I saw a bulletin once that listed the Rev. So and So as pastor and "the people" as the ministers. I wondered if it was true, if the power to care and to restore, to speak and to listen, were truly spread around as the bulletin claimed.

I've decided now that it doesn't quite matter. What matters is that they had set out for that destination and that they were on their way.

Two kinds of ministry . . .

Some of the thoughts in this article are expressed in this chart which contrasts two kinds of ministry. One is more private, where the minister has too much responsibility, has too little mandate to care for the poor, and is overworked and restless. The other is more public and has as its destination the sharing of the power to care, an orientation to the larger community and not just the parish-ioners, and an assumption that rest is possible along the way.

Public	**Private**
1. Upstream: Developing a community of ministers	Downstream: Aiding victims
2. Preventive: Forming a healing community	Medical: Healing wounds created by broken community
3. Community building in parish, family, neighborhood, state, world	Focus on members alone
4. Communities of partners	Communities of clients
5. Conflict open and expected, leading to forgiveness and change	Conflict actively minimized, leading to repression and stasis
6. Power purposefully in flux	Power bases solidified
7. Stories using biblical, developmental, sacramental language	Stories where time is disorganized and language is socially scientific
8. Outside: The church serves the world	Inside: The church gathers the wagons

How the "Impossible" Happened:
A Case Study in Inclusive Language

When as a senior pastor it became my responsibility to lead worship, it was easy to pray and preach in language that avoided the use of male pronouns or nouns. No one seemed to notice the absence, and I put effort into nonclumsy constructions. But it was hard to choose hymns, and I soon got sick of nature hymns. They may have been gender-free, but they were also too narrow a form of praise.

Then, a surprise. Something larger than my agenda intervened. I believe it was the Spirit calling me to a nonstrategic risk. I found myself talking over my problem with congregational leadership. The Board of Deacons created guidelines for me to follow.

For three months I would translate and photocopy hymns for worship use. The congregation would be informed that an experiment was going on and would be asked to comment following the service in a notebook placed in the narthex. The deacons would read the comments weekly and assure the congregation frequently that the pastor had agreed to congregational decision on the matter of language in hymns.

I never preached on the issue. I did teach a series of workshops. The sequence was called "The Many Names of God" and twenty-seven people attended four sessions. They included the two elderly women who were most offended by the change and the process. The curriculum included:

1. Biblical materials showing the many names and genders used to address God in the Bible.

2. An analysis of the Hebrew refusal to spell or speak the name of God—preferring breath to make the point.

3. A panel discussion with women from the congregation expressing offense *and* comfort in masculine usages.

4. A hymn-writing project where traditional and innovative forms were constructed by class participants (Many of these "translations" were used in future services).

5. A speaker on hymnody who demonstrated how frequently hymns (falsely considered eternal) have changed their language over the years for various social reasons.

The deacons argued that we had to listen to a new language before we could evaluate it. They were right: ears have to get accustomed to new sounds.

After the three-month trial period was over, two notebooks were full of ideas, suggestions, and comments. To everyone's surprise, most were positive.

The deacons then held an open meeting one Sunday after church, where they announced that a decision would be made to continue with the inclusive format or return to the traditional order. With the exception of one person—who eloquently pleaded for the "Our Father" in the Lord's Prayer—everyone present wanted to continue with many names for God in worship.

This first stage in our transition lasted about a year. Every Sunday God would be addressed in various ways, including Father, in prayers, hymns, and sermons. Soon we all began *not* paying attention to our unusual language. Worship, membership, and mission became subjects we discussed on a much larger scope than that of gender.

Then something interesting happened. A retired minister in the congregation, Rev. Phillip Ward, offered to help with the preparation of hymns for Sunday worship. He was a student of hymnody, a master with the English language, and he had a good ear. His wife had convinced him of the need for inclusive language, but his poet's ear wasn't pleased by his ethical decision. I was getting lazier and lazier as work in other directions piled up and thus was delighted by his offer.

He researched the history of every hymn in the *Pilgrim Hymnal*. He got copyrights on each hymn and guaranteed the public domain of those that had no copyright. He waded through other publications of women's groups around the country. He designed and printed an adapted version of the entire *Pilgrim Hymnal* in inclusive language. First Congregational in Amherst was his first customer; now 3,500 are in print.

Reprinted from *The Common Lot,* Summer 1986.

The Alban Institute:
an invitation to membership

The Alban Institute, begun in 1979, believes that the congregation is essential to the task of equipping the people of God to minister in the church and the world. A multi-denominational membership organization, the Institute provides on-site training, educational programs, consulting, research, and publishing for hundreds of churches across the country.

The Alban Institute invites you to be a member of this partnership of laity, clergy, and executives—a partnership that brings together people who are raising important questions about congregational life and people who are trying new solutions, making new discoveries, finding a new way of getting clear about the task of ministry. The Institute exists to provide you with the kinds of information and resources you need to support your ministries.

Join us now and enjoy these benefits:

Action Information, a highly respected journal published 6 times a year, to keep you up to date on current issues and trends.

Inside Information, Alban's quarterly newsletter, keeps you informed about research and other happenings around Alban. Available to members only.

Publication Discounts:

- ☐ 15% for Individual, Retired Clergy, and Seminarian Members
- ☐ 25% for congregational members
- ☐ 40% for Judicatory and Seminary Executive Members

Discounts on Training and Education Events

Write our Membership Department at the address below, or call us at (202) 244-7320 for more information about how to join The Alban Institute's growing membership, particularly about Congregational Membership in which 12 designated persons receive all benefits of membership.

The Alban Institute, Inc.
4125 Nebraska Avenue NW
Washington, DC 20016